ANSWERS
to 100
Frequently
Asked
Questions
about
Social Security
Retirement Benefits

Edited by JOHN WEBER

Welcome Rain Publishers
NEW YORK

Cover photo istock.com/BirdImages
Design by Smythtype Design

Welcome Rain Publisher LLC
217 Thompson Street, Suite 473
New York, NY 10012

ISBN 978-1-56649-400-7

Manufactured in the United States of America

Contents

Foreword

On the back cover we state: "For most people, Social Security is their largest financial asset, worth hundreds of thousands of dollars and indexed against increases in the cost of living."

We also say: "This book may be worth tens—or even hundreds—of thousands of dollars to you!"

Here's how:

The average monthly benefit in 2018 is $1,404. In order to generate that amount of income, you would have to have $842,400 in the bank earning a 2% annual return.

The average life expectancy of a 65-year-old is now 20 years. At the average of $1,404 a month, that comes to $336,960 in lifetime benefits. (And this does not include the increase from the cost-of-living adjustments.)

The two main ways you can lose Social Security retirement benefits are failure to apply for benefits that you are eligible for, and not maximizing your benefits.

Folks are almost always aware of the benefits due to them based on their own work record. Where the money is usually lost is on the auxiliary benefits, especially spousal (married people, divorced, and survivors). If this book makes you aware of your eligibility for benefits on someone else's work record, that could be very valuable information indeed!

About 40 percent of all retirees take their benefits at age 62, their first opportunity. They may not know that their monthly benefit will be 76 percent larger if they can hold off until they are 70. Waiting those eight years can generate an extra $1,000 a month for the rest of your life. If you live into your late eighties, or nineties (or your spouse does), waiting to collect can be one of the best "investments" you will ever make.

Introduction

"Life can only be understood backwards; but it must be lived forwards."
—Søren Kierkegaard

The most important decision you will make about Social Security is when to start taking retirement benefits. You can start as early as age 62 or delay until you are 70. The longer you wait, the larger your monthly payment—but you won't get as many payments.

So if you knew how long you were going to live, and there were no other considerations—such as a spouse—you could pretty easily do the math and figure out how to collect the most money during your retirement.

Unfortunately, we don't know how long we're going to live, so our most important decision about Social Security is based on a guess. (5.7% of the people who pay into Social Security die before collecting any benefits at all.) Factor in a spouse, and various strategies become possible, and the calculation becomes much more complicated. Factor in the determination of certain politicians to "reform" Social Security (by which they usually mean privatize it, or cut benefits*), and the calculation becomes daunting.

All of the answers you will find here are available on the Social Security Administration website (www.socialsecurity.gov); by phone (800-772-1213, Monday through Friday, 7 a.m. to 7 p.m.); or in a visit to your local SSA office, the location of which can be found on the website or by calling.

But if you've ever visited the SSA website, you've probably found the amount of information available overwhelming, disorganized, and mostly irrelevant to retirement issues (since the SSA is also responsible for Disability and Unemployment Insurance, Medicare, and Medicaid, among other Federal programs). If you've called their 800 number, you're probably still on hold.

The answers to your specific questions may not be here, but if you're reading this book, you are probably about to make several of the most important financial decisions of your life, and this book functions both as a primer and to dispel many of the common misconceptions people have about what Social Security is and how it works.

It is the editor's hope that, armed with the basic information contained here, you are better equipped to talk to the SSA and/or your financial advisor when the time comes, and pose the questions that are relevant to your own unique situation.

(Although, please note: While Social Security Administration employees are required to provide accurate information about the program, they are PROHIBITED from offering advice as to how or when you should claim benefits.)

(Disclaimer: This book is not published, authorized, or endorsed by the Social Security Administration.)

Although all the "answers" in this book are taken verbatim from the SSA website and publications, some of the "questions" have been "asked" by the editor. For instance, "What is the best age to start receiving retirement benefits?" does not appear among the SSA's FAQs. But, for example, SSA Publication No. 05-10147 begins with: "At Social Security, we're often asked, 'What is the best age to start receiving retirement benefits?'"

The contents of this book do not constitute legal or accounting advice. Everyone's situation is unique and you should consult with the SSA and/ or certified professionals before making important financial decisions.

*Under the guise of "closing loopholes," the Bipartisan Budget Act of 2015 decreased the benefits paid to retirees by an estimated $9 billion a year under the heading "Protecting Social Security." See Chapter 8, "Recent Changes." (A hypothetical question for the Congress of the United States: What shall we do to protect Social Security? Answer: Change the rules, cut benefits, and pay recipients less. We'll call it "Protecting Social Security." Works every time.)

Chapter One

Background

1. What are the purposes of Social Security?

2. What programs are included under Social Security?

3. How large is Social Security?

4. How do Social Security benefits and Supplemental Security Income (SSI) payments differ?

5. How is Social Security financed?

6. What are FICA and SECA taxes?

7. What is the current maximum amount of Taxable Earnings for Social Security this year? How has the Maximum Taxable Earnings changed over the years?

8. Do I "own" the money I pay in Social Security taxes?

9. What is the Old-Age and Survivors Insurance (OASI) Trust Fund?

1. What are the purposes of Social Security?

The Social Security Act and related laws establish a number of programs that have the following basic purposes:

- To provide for the material needs of individuals and families;
- To protect aged and disabled persons against the expenses of illness that may otherwise use up their savings;
- To keep families together; and
- To give children the chance to grow up healthy and secure.

2. What programs are included under Social Security?

The following programs are included:
- Retirement insurance;
- Survivors insurance;
- Disability insurance;
- Hospital and medical insurance for the aged, the disabled, and those with end-stage renal disease;
- Prescription Drug Benefit;
- Extra help with Medicare Prescription Drug Costs;
- Supplemental security income;
- Special Veterans Benefits;
- Unemployment insurance; and
- Public assistance and welfare services, including:
  - Temporary assistance for needy families;
  - Medical assistance;
  - Maternal and child health assistance;
  - Child support enforcement;
  - Family and child welfare services;
  - Food stamps; and
  - Energy assistance.

[EDITOR'S NOTE: This book deals ONLY with the first two programs listed above: RETIREMENT and SURVIVORS INSURANCE.]

---

3. How large is Social Security?

In 2017, over 62 million Americans will receive approximately $955 billion in Social Security benefits.

Per December 2016 Beneficiary Data

- **Retired workers:** 41.2 million/ $56 billion/ $1,360 average monthly benefit [see question #15 for current amount]
  Their dependents: 3 million/ $2 billion
- **Disabled workers:** 8.8 million/ $10.3 billion/ $1,171 average monthly benefit
  Their dependents: 1.8 million/ $0.65 billion
- **Survivors:** 6.1 million/ $6.8 billion

Social Security is the major source of income for most of the elderly.

- Nearly nine of ten individuals age 65 and older receive Social Security benefits.
- Social Security benefits represent about 34% of the income of the elderly.
- Among elderly Social Security beneficiaries, 48% of married couples and 71% of unmarried persons receive 50% or more of their income from Social Security.
- Among elderly Social Security beneficiaries, 21% of married couples and about 43% of unmarried persons rely on Social Security for 90% or more of their income.

Social Security provides more than just retirement benefits.

- Retired workers and their dependents account for 71% of total benefits paid.
- Survivors of deceased workers account for 13% of the total benefits paid.
  - About one in eight of today's 20-year-olds will die before reaching 67.
  - About 96% of persons aged 20–49 who worked in covered employment in 2016 have survivors insurance protection for their young children and the surviving spouse caring for the children.

An estimated 171 million workers are covered under Social Security.

- 51% of the workforce has no private pension coverage.
- 31% of workers report that they and/or their spouse have no savings set aside specifically for retirement.

In 1940, the life expectancy of a 65-year-old was almost 14 years; today it is about 20 years.

By 2035, the number of Americans 65 and older will increase from 48 million today to over 79 million.

There are currently 2.8 workers for each Social Security beneficiary. By 2035, there will be 2.2 covered workers for each beneficiary.

4. How do Social Security benefits and Supplemental Security Income (SSI) payments differ?

The two programs are financed differently.

- Employment taxes primarily finance Social Security retirement, survivors, and disability insurance benefits.
- Generally, we pay Social Security benefits to eligible workers and their families, based on the worker's earnings.
- Meanwhile, general taxes fund the SSI program, which serves the needy. SSI eligibility depends largely on limited income and resources.

5. How is Social Security financed?

Social Security is financed through a dedicated payroll tax. Employers and employees each pay 6.2 percent of wages up to the taxable maximum of $128,700 in 2018, while the self-employed pay 12.4 percent.

6. What are FICA and SECA taxes?

The law requires employers to withhold taxes from employee earnings to fund the Social Security and Medicare programs. These are called Federal Insurance Contributions Act (FICA) taxes. Your employer also pays a tax equal to the amount withheld from employee earnings.

The self-employed pay Self-Employed Contributions Act (SECA) taxes on net earnings. SECA taxes also fund Social Security and Medicare. The self-employed pay both the employee and the employer share of SECA. But the law permits them to deduct half of the self-employment tax as a business expense.

7. What is the current maximum amount of taxable earnings for Social Security this year? How has the Maximum Taxable Earnings changed over the years?

In 2018, the highest amount of earnings on which you must pay Social Security tax is $128,700. We raise this amount yearly to keep pace with increases in average wages. (There is no maximum earnings amount for Medicare tax. You must pay Medicare tax on all of your earnings.)

Maximum Taxable Earnings Each Year							
1937 – 50	$ 3,000	1982	$32,400	1998	$ 68,400	2014	$117,000
1951 – 54	3,600	1983	35,700	1999	72,600	2015	118,500
1955 – 58	4,200	1984	37,800	2000	76,200	2016	118,500
1959 – 65	4,800	1985	39,600	2001	80,400	2017	127,200
1966 – 67	6,600	1986	42,000	2002	84,900		
1968 – 71	7,800	1987	43,800	2003	87,000		
1972	9,000	1988	45,000	2004	87,900		
1973	10,800	1989	48,000	2005	90,000		
1974	13,200	1990	51,300	2006	94,200		
1975	14,100	1991	53,400	2007	97,500		
1976	15,300	1992	55,500	2008	102,000		
1977	16,500	1993	57,600	2009	106,800		
1978	17,700	1994	60,600	2010	106,800		
1979	22,900	1995	61,200	2011	106,800		
1980	25,900	1996	62,700	2012	110,100		
1981	29,700	1997	65,400	2013	113,700		

8. Do I "own" the money I pay in Social Security taxes?

We do not put the Social Security taxes you pay in a special account for you. They are used to pay benefits for people getting benefits today, just as your future benefits will be paid for by future workers.

9. What is the Old-Age and Survivors Insurance (OASI) Trust Fund?

The Social Security trust funds are financial accounts in the U.S. Treasury. There are two separate Social Security trust funds: the Old-Age and Survivors Insurance (OASI) Trust Fund pays retirement and survivors benefits; and the Disability Insurance (DI) Trust Fund pays disability benefits.

Social Security taxes and other income are deposited in these accounts, and Social Security benefits are paid from them. The only purposes for which these trust funds can be used are to pay benefits and program administrative costs.

The Social Security trust funds not needed in the current year to pay benefits and administrative costs are, by law, invested in special Treasury bonds that are guaranteed by the U.S. Government. A market rate of interest is paid to the trust funds on the bonds they hold, and when those bonds reach maturity or are needed to pay benefits, the Treasury redeems them.

[SEE ALSO question #97: "What is the current status of the Old-Age and Survivors (OASI) Trust Fund?"]

Chapter Two

Basics

10. What is a "mySocialSecurity" online account? What can I do with mySocialSecurity online account?

Setting up a mySocialSecurity online account:

11. What is the verification process you use to set up a mySocialSecurity online account?

12. Will the Identity Services Provider charge me to set up or use a mySocialSecurity online account?

13. Can I create a mySocialSecurity account if I have a security freeze or fraud alert on my credit report?

14. Why is Social Security asking for financial information online if I choose to add extra security to mySocialSecurity account?

[EDITOR'S NOTE: In an article about protection against identity theft in The New York Times *(dated October 30, 2017), its author recommends opening a mySocialSecurity account to "stop thieves from creating an account in your name, and redirecting benefits."]*

Benefit Basics:

15. What is the average monthly benefit for a retired worker?

16. What is the maximum Social Security retirement benefit payable?

10. What is a "mySocialSecurity" online account? What can I do with mySocialSecurity online account?

"mySocialSecurity" is a free online account that gives you quick and secure access to your personal Social Security information.

[EDITOR'S NOTE: If you value your time, setting up an account is a vastly superior alternative to going down to the local Social Security office or calling their 800 number (800-772-1213 or TTY 800-325-0778). You can set up an account by going to www.ssa.gov/myaccount.]

If you do NOT receive benefits you can:

- Get your Social Security Statement;
- Estimate your benefits;
- View your earnings record; and
- Apply for retirement and spouse's benefits.

If you receive benefits you can:

- Get your benefit verification letter;
- Check your payment information;
- Change your address or phone number; and
- Start or change direct deposit.

11. What is the verification process you use to set up a mySocialSecurity online account?

You must give us your identifying information and answer security questions to pass verification. First, we match the personal information you give us with the data we have in our records. Then, we use our "Identity Services Provider" to further verify your identity.

12. Will the Identity Services Provider charge me to set up or use a mySocialSecurity online account?

No, the "Identity Services Provider" will not charge you to set up a mySocialSecurity online account.

About the Identity Services Provider: The U.S. Social Security Administration uses an external data source, or what we refer to as an "Identity Services Provider," to help us verify the identity of our online customers and to prevent fraudulent access to our customers' sensitive personal information. Equifax is the Identity Services Provider that provides identity verification services to the Social Security Administration.

13. Can I create a mySocialSecurity account if I have a security freeze or a fraud alert on my credit report?

You cannot create a mySocialSecurity account online if you have a security freeze, fraud alert, or both on your credit report. You first must ask to have the freeze or alert removed.

To create a mySocialSecurity account in person without removing the security freeze or fraud alert, visit your local Social Security office.

14. Why is Social Security asking for financial information online if I choose to add extra security to mySocialSecurity account?

Social Security's new security process and federal guidelines require us to take extra measures to verify your identity online. It helps us ensure you are who you say you are and it protects your information.

15. What is the average monthly benefit for a retired worker?

The average monthly Social Security retirement benefit for 2018 is $1,404.

16. What is the maximum Social Security retirement benefit payable?

The maximum benefit depends on the age you retire. For example, if you retire at full retirement age in 2018, your maximum benefit would be $2,788. However, if you retire at age 62 in 2018, your maximum benefit would be $2,159. If you retire at age 70 in 2018, your maximum benefit would be $3,698.

Chapter Three

Eligibility

Please see Chapter 6, "Spouses, Dependents, and Survivors," for information concerning eligibility for benefits based on someone else's work record.

17. How do I earn Social Security credits and how many do I need to qualify for benefits?

18. Can work outside the United States help me qualify for Social Security benefits?

19. Can I contribute money to Social Security to earn extra credits?

20. How can I get a Social Security Statement that shows a record of my earnings and an estimate of my future benefits?

21. How do I correct my earnings record?

22. Can I get Social Security retirement benefits and military retirement benefits?

23. If I get Social Security disability benefits and I reach full retirement age, will I then receive retirement benefits?

24. Can non-citizens living in the United States receive Social Security benefits?

25. Can non-citizens living outside the United States receive Social Security benefits?

26. Can prisoners get Social Security payments?

27. What if I apply but Social Security decides I do not qualify for benefits? Will I receive a penalty or fine?

17. How do I earn Social Security credits and how many do I need to qualify for benefits?

We use your total yearly earnings to figure your Social Security credits. The amount needed for a credit in 2018 is $1,320. You can earn a maximum of four credits for any year. The amount needed to earn one credit increases automatically each year when average wages increase. You must earn a certain number of credits to qualify for Social Security benefits. The number of credits you need depends on your age when you apply and the type of benefit application. No one needs more than 40 credits for any Social Security benefit.

18. Can work outside the United States help me qualify for Social Security benefits?

The United States has Social Security agreements with more than two dozen foreign countries. The agreements have two main purposes:

- To eliminate dual Social Security payments and coverage; and
- To help fill gaps in protection for workers who have divided their careers between the United States and other countries.

19. Can I contribute money to Social Security to earn extra credits?

You cannot get more credits by voluntarily contributing money to Social Security. You can earn credits only by working in a job or your own business that is covered under Social Security.

20. How can I get a Social Security Statement that shows a record of my earnings and an estimate of my future benefits?

You can get your personal Social Security Statement online by using your mySocialSecurity account. If you don't yet have an account, you can easily create one. Your online Statement gives you secure and convenient access to your earnings records. It also shows estimates for retirement, disability, and survivors benefits you and your family may be eligible for.

We also mail paper Statements to workers age 60 and older three months before their birthday if they don't receive Social Security benefits and don't yet have a mySocialSecurity account. Workers who don't want to wait for their scheduled mailing can request their Social Security Statement by mail—please print and complete a "Request For Social Security Statement" (Form SSA-7004) and mail it to the address provided on the form.

You should receive your paper Social Security Statement in the mail in four to six weeks.

21. How do I correct my earnings record?

Ordinarily, you cannot correct your earnings after three years, three months, and 15 days from the end of the taxable year in which your wages were paid. However, you can correct your record after that length of time to:

- Confirm records with tax returns filed with the Internal Revenue Service;
- Correct errors due to employee omissions from processed employer reports or missing reports;
- Correct errors "on the face of the record," that is, errors we can find by examining our records of processed reports; and

- Include wages reported by an employer as paid to an individual, but not shown in our records.

To correct your Social Security earnings record, contact us at 1-800-772-1213 (TTY 1-800-325-0778). It will be helpful to have information such as Forms W-2, pay stubs, etc.

22. Can I get Social Security retirement benefits and military retirement benefits?

You can get both Social Security retirement benefits and military retirement. Generally, we do not reduce your Social Security benefits because of your military benefits.

23. If I get Social Security disability benefits and I reach full retirement age, will I then receive retirement benefits?

Social Security disability benefits automatically change to retirement benefits when disability beneficiaries become full retirement age. The law does not allow a person to receive both retirement and disability benefits on one earnings record at the same time.

24. Can non-citizens living in the United States receive Social Security benefits?

Yes, if they are lawfully in the United States and meet all eligibility requirements. Lawfully present non-citizens include, but are not limited to:

- Non-citizens lawfully admitted for permanent residence under the Immigration and Nationality Act (INA);
- Certain non-citizens admitted under other INA classifications that allow them to live and work in the United States;
- Non-citizens admitted under Family Unity or Immediate Relative provisions; and
- Other non-citizens who are fully insured for retirement, survivors, or disability benefits, and who continue to meet U.S. lawful presence requirements.

Non-citizens authorized to work in the United States who got a Social Security number after December 2003 can qualify for Social Security benefits.

---

25. Can non-citizens living outside the United States receive Social Security benefits?

In most cases, we stop payments to non-citizens after they are outside the United States for six calendar months in a row. If we stop your payments, we will not start them again until you return to the United States and remain for a full calendar month.

We may continue to pay benefits to non-citizens outside of the United States if they meet certain conditions. Use our Payments Abroad Screening Tool to find out if you can continue to get benefits while outside the United States.

For more information, see the SSA publication *Your Payments While You Are Outside the United States.*

26. Can prisoners get Social Security payments?

Social Security prohibits payments to most prisoners.

We will suspend your Social Security benefits if you are confined to a jail, prison, or other penal institution for more than 30 continuous days due to a criminal conviction. Although you can't get monthly Social Security benefits while you are confined, we will continue to pay benefits to your dependent spouse or children as long as they remain eligible.

27. What if I apply but Social Security decides I do not qualify for benefits? Will I receive a penalty or fine?

No, you will not receive a penalty or fine if Social Security denies your claim because you do not qualify for benefits. Likewise, if you appeal that decision or apply again, you will not receive a penalty or a fine.

Chapter Four

When to Apply

[EDITOR'S NOTE: Social Security provides several very helpful "Calculators" to help you decide when to start taking your retirement benefits on their website: https://www.ssa.gov/planners/ benefitcalculators.html.]

28. What is the Social Security Retirement Age Calculator?

29. What is the Social Security Life Expectancy Calculator?

30. How does the Social Security Retirement Estimator work?

[EDITOR'S NOTE: Other Calculators compare the effect on your benefit amount if you retire early or delay collecting; the effect of early retirement on the benefit for your spouse; and various other special circumstances such as the effects of the Windfall Elimination Provision (which deals with pensions based on work that was not covered by Social Security) and the Government Pension Offset.]

FAQs:

31. When can I get Social Security retirement benefits?

32. What is full retirement age and when is it increasing?

33. What are Delayed Retirement Credits and how do they increase my monthly payments?

34. Can I retire anytime, or only on my birthdays?

35. What's the best age to start receiving retirement benefits?

36. How do you figure out how much I will get?

28. What is the Social Security Retirement Age Calculator?

The Full Retirement Age is increasing.

Full retirement age (also called "normal retirement age") had been 65 for many years. However, beginning with people born in 1938 or later, that age gradually increases until it reaches 67 for people born after 1959.

The 1983 Social Security Amendments included a provision for raising the full retirement age beginning with people born in 1938 or later. The Congress cited improvements in the health of older people and increases in average life expectancy as primary reasons for increasing the normal retirement age.

NOTE: If you were born on January 1st of any year you should refer to the previous year.

[EDITOR'S NOTE: Available on the Social Security website, this calculator is simple to use: Just fill in when you were born and it tells you what your Full Retirement Age is. You can retire as early as age 62, or as late as age 70 regardless of what your Full Retirement Age is. The earlier you retire, the less your monthly payment; the later you retire, the larger your monthly payment—but you won't get as many.]

Link to Retirement Age Calculator
https://www.ssa.gov/planners/retire/ageincrease.html

29. What is the Social Security Life Expectancy Calculator?

When you are considering when to collect retirement benefits, one important factor to take into account is how long you might live. According to data compiled by the Social Security Administration:

- A man reaching age 65 today can expect to live, on average, until age 84.3.
- A woman turning age 65 today can expect to live, on average, until age 86.6.

And those are just averages. About one out of every four 65-year-olds today will live past age 90, and one out of 10 will live past age 95.

Want to know your life expectancy? You can use our simple Life Expectancy Calculator to get a rough estimate of how long you (or your spouse) may live. Knowing this information can help you make a more informed choice regarding when to collect Social Security retirement benefits.

Link to Life Expectancy Calculator
https://www.ssa.gov/OACT/population/longevity.html

---

30. How does the Social Security Retirement Estimator work?

How the Retirement Estimator works

The Retirement Estimator gives estimates based on your actual Social Security earnings record. Please keep in mind that these are just estimates. We can't provide your actual benefit amount until you apply for benefits. And that amount may differ from the estimates provided because:

- Your earnings may increase or decrease in the future.
- After you start receiving benefits, they will be adjusted for cost-of-living increases.
- Your estimated benefits are based on current law. The law governing benefit amounts may change because, by 2034, the payroll taxes

collected will be enough to pay only about 79 cents for each dollar of scheduled benefits.

- Your benefit amount may be affected by military service, railroad employment, or pensions earned through work on which you did not pay Social Security tax.

Who can use the Retirement Estimator

You can use the Retirement Estimator if...

- You have enough Social Security credits at this time to qualify for benefits; and
- You are *not*:
  - currently receiving benefits on your own Social Security record;
  - waiting for a decision about your application for benefits or Medicare;
  - age 62 or older and receiving benefits on another Social Security record; or
  - eligible for a pension based on work not covered by Social Security (for more go to *https://www.ssa.gov/planners/retire/gpo-wep.html*).

If you are currently receiving only Medicare benefits, you can still get an estimate. For more information go to this link *https://www.ssa.gov/pubs/EN-05-10529.pdf* for our publication *Retirement Information for Medicare Beneficiaries.*

If you cannot use the Retirement Estimator or you want a survivors or disability benefit estimate, please use one of our other benefit Calculators.

Link to Social Security Retirement Estimator
https://secure.ssa.gov/acu/ACU_KBA/main.jsp?URL=/apps8z/ARPI/main.jsp?locale=en&LVL=4

31. When can I get Social Security retirement benefits?

You can begin getting Social Security retirement benefits as early as age 62. But we will reduce your benefits by as much as 30 percent below what you would get if you waited to retire until your full retirement age. If you wait until your full retirement age (66 for most people), you will get your full benefit. You also can wait until age 70 to start your benefits. Then, we will increase your benefit because you earned "delayed retirement credits."

32. What is Full Retirement Age and when is it increasing?

Age to Receive Full Social Security Benefits (Called "full retirement age" or "normal retirement age.")	
Year of Birth *	Full Retirement Age
1937 or earlier	65
1938	65 and 2 months
1939	65 and 4 months
1940	65 and 6 months
1941	65 and 8 months
1942	65 and 10 months
1943–1954	66
1955	66 and 2 months
1956	66 and 4 months
1957	66 and 6 months
1958	66 and 8 months
1959	66 and 10 months
1960 and later	67

*If you were born on January 1st of any year you should refer to the previous year. If you were born on the 1st of the month, we figure your benefit (and your full retirement age) as if your birthday was in the previous month.

33. What are delayed Retirement Credits and how do they increase my monthly payments?

Social Security retirement benefits are increased by a certain percentage (depending on date of birth) if you delay your retirement beyond full retirement age.

The benefit increase no longer applies when you reach age 70, even if you continue to delay taking benefits.

Increase for Delayed Retirement		
Year of Birth*	Yearly Rate of Increase	Monthly Rate of Increase
1933 – 1934	5.5%	11/24 of 1%
1935 – 1936	6.0%	1/2 of 1%
1937 – 1938	6.5%	13/24 of 1%
1939 – 1940	7.0%	7/12 of 1%
1941 – 1942	7.5%	5/8 of 1%
1943 or later	8.0%	2/3 of 1%
* If you were born on January 1st, you should refer to the rate of increase for the previous year.		

34. Can I retire anytime, or only on my birthdays?

[EDITOR'S NOTE: You can retire anytime and apply anytime. Here is how your benefits will be affected month-by-month if you were born between 1943–1954.]

How Early Retirement Affects Your Social Security Benefits

Early Retirement Age	Benefit	Early Retirement Age	Benefit
62	75.0%	64 + 6 months	90.0
62 + 1 month	75.4	64 + 7 months	90.6
62 + 2 months	75.8	64 + 8 months	91.1
62 + 3 months	76.3	64 + 9 months	91.7
62 + 4 months	76.7	64 + 10 months	92.2
62 + 5 months	77.1	64 + 11 months	92.8
62 + 6 months	77.5	65	93.3
62 + 7 months	77.9	65 + 1 month	93.9
62 + 8 months	78.3	65 + 2 months	94.4
62 + 9 months	78.8	65 + 3 months	95.0
62 + 10 months	79.2	65 + 4 months	95.6
62 + 11 months	79.6	65 + 5 months	96.1
63	80.0	65 + 6 months	96.7
63 + 1 month	80.6	65 + 7 months	97.2
63 + 2 months	81.1	65 + 8 months	97.8
63 + 3 months	81.7	65 + 9 months	98.3
63 + 4 months	82.2	65 + 10 months	98.9
63 + 5 months	82.8	65 + 11 months	99.4
63 + 6 months	83.3	66	100.0
63 + 7 months	83.9		
63 + 8 months	84.4		
63 + 9 months	85.0		
63 + 10 months	85.6		
63 + 11 months	86.1		
64	86.7		
64 + 1 month	87.2		
64 + 2 months	87.8		
64 + 3 months	88.3		
64 + 4 months	88.9		
64 + 5 months	89.4		

How Delayed Retirement Affects Your Social Security Benefits			
Delayed Retirement Age	**Benefit**	**Delayed Retirement Age**	**Benefit**
66	100%	69	124.0%
66 + 1 month	100.7%	69 + 1 month	124.7%
66 + 2 months	101.3%	69 + 2 months	125.3%
66 + 3 months	102.0%	69 + 3 months	126.0%
66 + 4 months	102.7%	69 + 4 months	126.7%
66 + 5 months	103.3%	69 + 5 months	127.3%
66 + 6 months	104.0%	69 + 6 months	128.0%
66 + 7 months	104.7%	69 + 7 months	128.7%
66 + 8 months	105.3%	69 + 8 months	129.3%
66 + 9 months	106.0%	69 + 9 months	130.0%
66 + 10 months	106.7%	69 + 10 months	130.7%
66 + 11 months	107.3%	69 + 11 months	131.3%
67	108.0%	70 or later	132.0%
67 + 1 month	108.7%		
67 + 2 months	109.3%		
67 + 3 months	110.0%		
67 + 4 months	110.7%		
67 + 5 months	111.3%		
67 + 6 months	112.0%		
67 + 7 months	112.7%		
67 + 8 months	113.3%		
67 + 9 months	114.0%		
67 + 10 months	114.7%		
67 + 11 months	115.3%		
68	116.0%		
68 + 1 month	116.7%		
68 + 2 months	117.3%		
68 + 3 months	118.0%		
68 + 4 months	118.7%		
68 + 5 months	119.3%		
68 + 6 months	120.0%		
68 + 7 months	120.7%		
68 + 8 months	121.3%		
68 + 9 months	122.0%		
68 + 10 months	122.7%		
68 + 11 months	123.3%		

35. What's the best age to start receiving retirement benefits?

At Social Security, we're often asked, "What's the best age to start receiving retirement benefits?" The answer is that there is no one "best age" for everyone and, ultimately, it's your choice. The most important thing is to make an informed decision. Base your decision about when to apply for benefits on your individual and family circumstances. We hope the following information will help you understand how Social Security fits into your retirement decision.

Your decision is a personal one.

Would it be better for you to start getting benefits early with a smaller monthly amount for more years, or wait for a larger monthly payment over a shorter timeframe? The answer is personal and depends on several factors, such as your current cash needs, your current health, and family longevity. Also, consider if you plan to work in retirement and if you have other sources of retirement income. You must also study your future financial needs and obligations, and calculate your future Social Security benefit. We hope you'll weigh all the facts carefully before making the crucial decision about when to begin receiving Social Security benefits. This decision affects the monthly benefit you will receive for the rest of your life, and may affect benefit protection for your survivors.

Your monthly retirement benefit will be higher if you delay starting it.

Your full retirement age varies based on the year you were born. You can visit *www.socialsecurity.gov/planners/retire/ageincrease.html* to find your full retirement age. We calculate your basic Social Security benefit—the amount you would receive at your full retirement age— based on your lifetime earnings. However, the actual amount you receive each month depends on when you start receiving benefits. You can start your retirement benefit at any point from age 62 up until age 70, and your benefit will be higher the longer you delay starting it. This adjustment is usually permanent: it sets the base for the benefits you'll get for the rest of your life. You'll get annual cost-of-living adjustments and, depending on your work history, may receive higher benefits if you continue to work.

The following chart shows an example of how your monthly benefit increases if you delay when you start receiving benefits.

Monthly Benefit Amounts Differ Based on the Age You Decide to Start Receiving Benefits

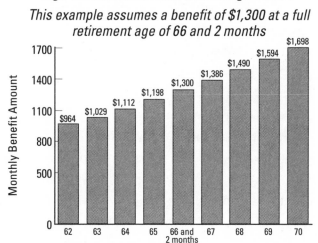

This example assumes a benefit of $1,300 at a full retirement age of 66 and 2 months

Let's say you turn 62 in 2017, your full retirement age is 66 and 2 months, and your monthly benefit starting at that age is $1,300. If you start getting benefits at age 62, we'll reduce your monthly benefit 25.8 percent to $964 to account for the longer time you receive benefits. This decrease is usually permanent.

If you choose to delay getting benefits until age 70, you would increase your monthly benefit to $1,698. This increase is a result of delayed retirement credits you earn for your decision to postpone receiving benefits past your full retirement age. The benefit at age 70 in this example is 76 percent more than the benefit you would receive each month if you start getting benefits at age 62—a difference of $734 each month.

Retirement may be longer than you think.

When thinking about retirement, be sure to plan for the long term. Many of us will live much longer that the "average" retiree, and most women live longer than men. More than one in three 65-year-olds today will live to age 90, and more than one in seven will live to age 95. Social Security benefits, which last as long as you live, provide valuable protection against outliving savings and other sources of retirement income. Again, you'll want to choose a retirement age based on your circumstances so you'll have enough income when you need it.

Married couples have two lives to plan for.

Your spouse may be eligible for a benefit based on your work record, and it's important to consider Social Security protection for widowed spouses. After all, married couples at age 65 today would typically have a 50–50 chance that one member of the couple will live beyond age 90. If you are the higher earner, and you delay starting your retirement benefit, it will result in higher monthly benefits for the rest of your life and higher survivor protection for your spouse, if you die first.

When you are receiving retirement benefits, your children can also be eligible for a benefit on your work record if they're under age 18 or if they have a disability that began before age 22.

You can keep working.

When you reach your full retirement age, you can work and earn as much as you want and still get your full Social Security benefit payment. If you're younger than full retirement age and if your earnings exceed certain dollar amounts, some of your benefits payments during the year will be withheld.

That doesn't mean you must try to limit your earnings. If we withhold some of your benefits because you continue to work, we'll pay you a higher monthly benefit when you reach your full retirement age. So, if you work and earn more than the exempt amount, it won't, on average, decrease the total value of your lifetime benefits from Social Security—and can increase them.

Here is how this works: When you reach full retirement age, we'll recalculate your benefit to give you credit for months you didn't get a benefit because of your earnings. In addition, as long as you continue to work and receive benefits, we'll check your record every year to see whether the extra earnings will increase your monthly benefit.

Don't forget Medicare.

If you plan to delay receiving benefits because you're working, you'll still need to sign up for Medicare three months before reaching age 65. If you don't enroll in Medicare medical insurance or prescription drug coverage when you're first eligible, it can be delayed, and you may have to pay a late enrollment penalty for as long as you have coverage. You can find more detailed information about Medicare on our website at *www.socialsecurity.gov/medicare.*

More resources.

You can estimate benefit amounts and find more information to help you decide when to start receiving retirement benefits by using our benefits planners at *www.socialsecurity.gov/planners.* You can also use our Retirement Estimator at *www.socialsecurity.gov/estimator* or create a mySocialSecurity account and get your Social Security Statement at *www.socialsecurity.gov/myaccount.* Both tools provide retirement benefit estimates based on your actual earnings record.

When you're ready for benefits, you can also apply online at *www.socialsecurity.gov/applyforbenefits.* You can continue to work and still receive retirement benefits. If you want more information about how your earnings affect your retirement benefits, read *How Work Affects Your Benefits* (Publication No. 05-10069). This pamphlet has the current annual and monthly earning limits.

Contacting Social Security.

The most convenient way to contact us anytime, anywhere, is to visit *www.socialsecurity.gov.* There, you can: apply for benefits; open a mySocialSecurity account, which you can use to review your Social Security Statement, verify your earnings, print a benefit verification letter, change your direct deposit information, request a replacement Medicare card, and get a replacement 1099/1042S; obtain valuable information; find publications; get answers to frequently asked questions; and much more.

If you don't have access to the internet, we offer many automated services by telephone, 24 hours a day, 7 days a week. Call us toll-free at 1-800-772-1213 or at our TTY number, 1-800-325-0778, if you're deaf or hard of hearing.

If you need to speak to a person, we can answer your calls from 7 a.m. to 7 p.m., Monday through Friday. We ask for your patience during busy periods since you may experience a higher than usual rate of busy signals and longer hold times to speak to us. We look forward to serving you.

---

36. How do you figure out how much I will get?

As you make plans for your retirement, you may ask, "How much will I get from Social Security?" You can use the Retirement Estimator at *www.socialsecurity.gov/estimator* to find out how much you might receive.

Many people wonder how their benefit is figured. Social Security benefits are based on your lifetime earnings. Your actual earnings are adjusted or "indexed" to account for changes in average wages since the year the earnings were received. Then Social Security calculates your average indexed monthly earnings during the 35 years in which you earned the most. We apply a formula to these earnings and arrive at your basic benefit, or "primary insurance amount" (PIA). This is how much you would receive at your full retirement age—65 or older, depending on your date of birth.

Factors that can change the amount of your retirement benefit:

- **You choose to get benefits before your full retirement age.** You can begin to receive Social Security benefits as early as age 62, but at a reduced rate. Your basic benefit will be reduced by a certain percentage if you retire before reaching full retirement age.
- **You are eligible for cost-of-living benefit increases starting with the year you become age 62.** This is true even if you do not get benefits until your full retirement age or even age 70. Cost-of-living increases are added to your benefit beginning with the year you reach 62 up to the year you start receiving benefits.
- **You delay your retirement past your full retirement age.** Social Security benefits are increased by a certain percentage (depending on your date of birth) if you delay receiving benefits until after your full retirement age. If you do so, your benefit amount will be increased until you start taking benefits or you reach age 70.

Chapter Five

Applying

37. How far in advance can I apply for Social Security retirement benefits?

38. How do I apply for Social Security retirement benefits?

39. What does the Application for Retirement Insurance Benefits look like?

37. How far in advance can I apply for Social Security retirement benefits?

You can apply for Social Security retirement benefits when you are at least 61 years and 9 months of age.

You should apply three months before you want your benefits to start.

Even if you are not ready to retire, you still should sign up for Medicare three months before your 65th birthday.

38. How do I apply for Social Security retirement benefits?

You should apply for retirement benefits three months before you want your payments to start. The easiest and most convenient way to apply for retirement benefits is by using our online application.

We may need to see certain documents in order to pay benefits. If you apply online, a list of documents we need to see will appear at the end of the application, along with instructions on where to submit them. The documents we may ask for are:

- Your original birth certificate or other proof of birth [see below #1]. (You may also submit a copy of your birth certificate certified by the issuing agency);
- Proof of U.S. citizenship or lawful alien status if you were not born in the United States [see below #2];
- A copy of your U.S. military service paper(s) (e.g., DD-214-Certificate of Release or Discharge from Active Duty) if you had military service before 1968 [see below #3]; and
- A copy of your W-2 form(s) [see below #4] and/or self-employment tax return [see below #5] for last year.

You can also apply:

By phone: Call us at 1-800-772-1213 (TTY 1-800-325-0778), Monday through Friday from 7 a.m. to 7 p.m.; or

In person: Visit your local Social Security Office. (Call first to make an appointment.)

If you do not live in the U.S. or one of its territories you can also: Contact the nearest U.S. Social Security office, U.S. Embassy, or consulate.

NOTES on documentation:

1. (Proof of birth.)
If we ask for proof of your age, you must show us a birth certificate or religious record showing your age that was made before you were age 5 if one was established. This is our preferred proof of age.

If a public or religious record was not made before you were age 5, you must show us at least two other documents you may have that prove your age, such as a:

- birth certificate recorded after you were age 5,
- school record,
- State census record,
- vaccination record,
- insurance policy, OR
- hospital admission record, etc.

Please show us the oldest of these documents.

NOTE: We must see the original document(s) or copies certified by the agency that issued them. We cannot accept photocopies or notarized copies. We will return all your documents to you unless you specifically tell us otherwise. If you have the documents we need, you should submit them as soon as possible. If you don't have all the documents, you should submit any documents you do have. We will help you get the other documents.

IMPORTANT: If you mail any documents to us, we must have your Social Security Number so we can match them with your application. Please write your Social Security Number on a separate sheet of paper and include it in the mailing envelope along with your documents.

DO NOT write anything on your original documents. If you do not want to mail your documents, you may bring them to the Social Security office where we will examine and return them to you. Or, if a later office visit becomes necessary, you may bring them with you at that time.

CAUTION: Do not mail foreign birth records or any Department of Homeland Security (DHS) documents to us—especially those you are required to keep with you at all times. These documents are extremely difficult, time-consuming, and expensive to replace if lost. Some cannot be replaced. Instead, bring them to the Social Security office where we will examine and return them to you.

2. (Proof of citizenship or lawful alien status.)
We can accept most documents that show you were born in the U.S.

If you are a U.S. Citizen born outside the U.S., we need to see a document such as a:

- U.S. consular report of birth,
- U.S. passport,
- Certificate of Naturalization, or
- Certificate of Citizenship.

If you are not a U.S. citizen, we need to see your Department of Homeland Security (DHS) documents, including form I-551 (Permanent Resident Card, commonly known as a "Green Card") to verify your 9-digit Alien Registration Number (A-Number). If you have a DHS form I-94, Admission-Departure Record, we need to see that document to verify your 11-digit Admission Number.

We must see the original document(s), or copies certified by the agency that issued them. We cannot accept documents if they have expired. We cannot accept photocopies or notarized copies. We will return all documents to you unless you specifically tell us otherwise. If you have the documents we need, you should submit them as soon as possible. If you don't have all the documents, you should submit any documents you do have. We will help you get the other documents.

NOTE: If you mail any documents to us, we must have your Social Security Number so that we can match them with your application. Please write your Social Security Number on a separate sheet of paper and include it in the mailing envelope along with your documents.

IMPORTANT: Do not write anything on your original documents. If you do not want to mail your documents, you may bring them to the Social Security office where we will examine and return them to you. Or, if a later office visit becomes necessary, you may bring them with you at that time.

CAUTION: Do not mail foreign birth records or any Department of Homeland Security (DHS) documents to us, especially those you are required to keep with you at all times. These documents are extremely difficult, time-consuming, and expensive to replace if lost. Some cannot be replaced. Instead, bring them to your local Social Security office where we will examine and return them to you.

3. (Proof of U.S. military service.)

Proof of U.S. Military Service includes your military service papers, such as your Form DD-214 - Certificate of Release or Discharge from Active Duty. If you served two or more periods of active duty that were separated by at least one month, we will need to see the DD-214s that show the beginning and ending dates of active duty for each period.

For your convenience, we can accept photocopies of your military service papers. We will return all documents and photocopies to you unless you specifically tell us otherwise. If you have the documents we need, you should submit them as soon as possible. If you don't have all the documents, you should still submit any documents you do have. We will help you get the other documents after we receive your application.

NOTE: If you mail any documents to us, we must have your Social Security Number so we can match them with your claim. Please write your Social Security Number on a separate sheet of paper and include it in the mailing envelope along with your documents.

IMPORTANT: Do not write anything on your original documents. If you do not want to mail your documents, you may bring them to the Social Security office where we will examine and return them to you. Or, if a later office visit becomes necessary, you may bring them with you at that time.

4. (Proof of employment: W-2.)
If you worked for someone else last year, we need to see your Form W-2. For the current year, we can accept a statement of your earnings from your employer, as long as Social Security earnings (also known as FICA or OASDI earnings) are shown separately.

For your convenience, we can accept photocopies of your W-2 forms. We will return all documents and photocopies to you unless you specifically tell us otherwise. If you have the documents we need, you should submit them as soon as possible. If you don't have all the documents, you should submit any documents you do have. We will help you get the other documents.

NOTE: If you mail any documents to us, we must have your Social Security Number so we can match them with your claim. Please write your Social Security Number on a separate sheet of paper and include it in the mailing envelope along with your documents.

IMPORTANT: Do not write anything on your original documents. If you do not want to mail your documents, you may bring them to the Social Security office where we will examine and return them to you. Or, if a later office visit becomes necessary, you may bring them with you at that time.

5. (Proof of self-employment.)
If you were self-employed last year, we need to see a copy of Schedule C and SE from your tax return.

For your convenience, we can accept photocopies of your self-employment tax returns. We will return all documents and photocopies to you unless you specifically tell us otherwise. If you have the documents we need, you should submit them as soon as possible. If you don't have all the documents, you should submit any documents you do have. We will help you get the other documents.

NOTE: If you mail any documents to us, we must have your Social Security Number so we can match them with your claim. Please write your Social Security Number on a separate sheet of paper and include it in the mailing envelope along with your documents.

IMPORTANT: Do not write anything on your original documents. If you do not want to mail your documents, you may bring them to the Social Security office where we will examine and return them to you. Or, if a later office visit becomes necessary, you may bring them with you at that time.

39. What does the Application for Retirement Benefits look like?

SAMPLE ONLY—DO NOT USE FOR SUBMISSION!

Form SSA-1-BK (03-2017) UF

Application for Retirement Insurance Benefits

I apply for all insurance benefits for which I am eligible under Title II (Federal Old-Age, Survivors, and Disability Insurance) and Part A of Title XVIII (Health Insurance for the Aged and Disabled) of the Social Security Act, as presently amended.

☐ Supplement, if you have already completed an application entitled "APPLICATION FOR WIFE'S OR HUSBAND'S INSURANCE BENEFITS", you need complete only the circled items. All other claimants must complete the entire form.

①ⓐ PRINT your name: FIRST NAME, MIDDLE INITIAL, LAST NAME
    ⓑ check (x) whether you are ☐ Male ☐ Female

② Enter your Social Security number:

Answer question 3 if English is not your language preference. Otherwise, go to item 4.

3. Enter the language you prefer to: Speak _____ Write _____

4. (a) Enter your date of birth: Month, Day, Year _____
    (b) Enter name of city and state, or foreign country where you were born. _____
    (c) Was a public record of your birth made before you were age 5? ☐ Yes ☐ No ☐ Unknown
    (d) Was a religious record of your birth made before you were age 5? ☐ Yes ☐ No ☐ Unknown

5. (a) Are you a U.S. citizen? ☐ Yes (Go to item 7.) ☐ No (Go to item (b).)
    (b) Are you an alien lawfully present in the U.S.? ☐ Yes (Go to item (c).) ☐ No (Go to item 6.)
    (c) When were you lawfully admitted to the U.S.? _____

6. Enter your full name at birth if different from item 1(a). FIRST NAME, MIDDLE INITIAL, LAST NAME

_____

7. (a) Have you used any other name(s)? ☐ Yes (Go to item (b).) ☐ No (Go to item 8.)
    (b) Other name(s) used. _____

8. (a) Have you used any other Social Security number(s)? ☐ Yes (Go to item (b).) ☐ No (Go to item 9.)
   (b) Enter Social Security number(s) used. _____

Do not answer question 9 if you are one year past full retirement age or older; go to question 10.

9. (a) Are you, or during the past 14 months have you been, unable to work because of illness, injuries, or conditions? ☐ Yes ☐ No
   (b) If "Yes", enter the date you became unable to work. MONTH, DAY, YEAR _____

10. (a) Have you (or has someone on your behalf) ever filed an application for Social Security, Supplemental Security Income, or hospital or medical insurance under Medicare?
   ☐ Yes (If "Yes," answer (b) and (c).) ☐ No (If "No," go to item 11.)
   ☐ Unknown (If "Unknown," go to item 11.)
   (b) Enter the name of the person(s) on whose Social Security record you filed other application.
   FIRST NAME, MIDDLE INITIAL, LAST NAME_____
   (c) Enter Social Security number(s) of person named in (b).
   (If unknown, so indicate.) _____

11. (a) Were you in the active military or naval service (including Reserve or National Guard active duty or active duty for training) after September 7, 1939 and before 1968?
   ☐ Yes (If "Yes," answer (b) and (c).) ☐ No (If "No," go to item 12.)
   (b) Enter date(s) of service:
   From (Month, Year) _____ To (Month, Year) _____
   © Have you ever been (or will you be) eligible for monthly benefits from a military or civilian Federal agency? (Include Veterans Administration benefits only if you waived Military retirement pay). ☐ Yes ☐ No

12. Did you or your spouse (or prior spouse) work in the railroad industry for 5 years or more?
   ☐ Yes ☐ No

13. (a) Do you (or your spouse) have Social Security credits (for example based on work or residence) under another country's Social Security system?
   ☐ Yes (If "Yes," answer (b) and (c).) ☐ No (If "No," go to item 14.)
   (b) List the country(ies): _____
   (c) Are you (or your spouse) filing for foreign Social Security benefits? ☐ Yes ☐ No

Answer question 14 only if you were born January 2, 1924, or later. Otherwise go to question 15.

(14). (a) Are you entitled to, or do you expect to be entitled to, a pension or annuity (or a lump sum in place of a pension or annuity) based on your work after 1956 not covered by Social Security?

☐ Yes (If "Yes," answer (b) and (c).)   ☐ No (If "No," go on to item 15.)

(b) I became entitled, or expect to become entitled, beginning MONTH/ YEAR _____

(c) I became eligible, or expect to become eligible, beginning MONTH/YEAR _____

I agree to promptly notify the Social Security Administration if I become entitled to a pension, an annuity, or a lump sum payment based on my employment not covered by Social Security, or if such pension or annuity stops.

15. Have you been married? ☐ Yes (If "Yes," answer item 16.) ☐ No (If "No," go to item 17.)

16. (a) Give the following information about your current marriage. If not currently married, write "None." Go on to item 16 (b).

Spouse's name (including maiden name) _____

When (Month, day, year) _____

Where (Name of City and State)_____

How marriage ended (if still in effect, write "Not Ended.") _____

When (Month, day, year) _____

Where (Name of City and State) _____

Marriage performed by ☐ Clergyman or public official ☐ Other (Explain in "Remarks")

Spouse's date of birth (or age) _____

If spouse deceased, give date of death _____

Spouse's Social Security number (if none or unknown, so indicate) _____

(b) Enter information about any other marriage if you:

- Had a marriage that lasted at least 10 years; or
- Had a marriage that ended due to death of your spouse, regardless of duration; or
- Were divorced, remarried the same individual within the year immediately following the year of the divorce, and the combined period of marriage totaled 10 years or more.

Use the "Remarks" space to enter additional marriage information. If none, write "None." Go on to item 16 (c) if you have a child(ren) who is under age 16 or disabled or handicapped (age 16 or over and disability began before age 22); and you are divorced from the child's other parent, who is now deceased, and the marriage lasted less than 10 years.

Spouse's name (including maiden name) _____

When (Month, day, year) _____

Where (Name of City and State)_____

How marriage ended (if still in effect, write "Not Ended.") _____

When (Month, day, year) _____

Where (Name of City and State) _____

Marriage performed by ☐ Clergyman or public official ☐ Other (Explain in "Remarks")

Spouse's date of birth (or age) _____

If spouse deceased, give date of death _____

Spouse's Social Security number (if none or unknown, so indicate)_____

(c) Enter information about any marriage if you:

- Have a child(ren) who is under age 16 or disabled or handicapped (age 16 or over and disability began before age 22); and
- Were married less than 10 years to the child's mother or father, who is now deceased; and
- The marriage ended in divorce. If none, write "None."

To whom married_____

When (Month, day, year) _____

Where (Name of City and State)_____

How marriage ended (if still in effect, write "Not Ended.") _____

When (Month, day, year) _____

Where (Name of City and State) _____

Marriage performed by ☐ Clergyman or public official ☐ Other (Explain in "Remarks")

Spouse's date of birth (or age) _____

If spouse deceased, give date of death _____

Spouse's Social Security number (if none or unknown, so indicate) _____

Use the "Remarks" space on page 54 for marriage continuation or explanation.

If your claim for retirement benefits is approved, your children (including adopted children and stepchildren) or dependent grandchildren (including step grandchildren) may be eligible for benefits based on your earnings record.

(17) List below FULL NAME OF ALL your children (including adopted children, and stepchildren) or dependent grandchildren (including step grandchildren) who are now or were in the past 6 months UNMARRIED and:

- UNDER AGE 18
- AGE 18 to 19 AND ATTENDING SECONDARY SCHOOL OR ELEMENTARY SCHOOL FULL-TIME
- DISABLED OR HANDICAPPED (age 18 or over and disability began before age 22)

Also list any student who is between the ages of 18 to 23 if such student was both: Previously entitled to Social Security benefits on any Social Security record for August 1981; and 2. In full-time attendance at a post-secondary school.

(IF THERE ARE NO SUCH CHILDREN, WRITE "NONE" BELOW AND GO ON TO ITEM 18.)

----

18. (a) Did you have wages or self-employment income covered under Social Security in all years from 1978 through last year? ☐ Yes (If "Yes," go to item 19.)   ☐ No (If "No," answer item (b).)

(b) List the years from 1978 through last year in which you did not have wages or self-employment income covered under Social Security. _____

----

⑲ Enter below the names and addresses of all the persons, companies, or government agencies for whom you have worked this year, last year, and the year before last. IF NONE, WRITE "NONE" BELOW AND GO ON TO ITEM 20.

NAME AND ADDRESS OF EMPLOYER (If you had more than one employer, please list them in order beginning with your last (most recent) employer.)

Work Began (Month/Year)_____
Work Ended (If still working, show "Not Ended") _____

Work Began (Month/Year)_____
Work Ended (If still working, show "Not Ended") _____

Work Began (Month/Year)_____
Work Ended (If still working, show "Not Ended") _____

Work Began (Month/Year)_____
Work Ended (If still working, show "Not Ended") _____

If you need more space, use "Remarks".

20. May we ask your employers for wage information needed to process your claim? ☐ Yes ☐ No

21. THIS ITEM MUST BE COMPLETED, EVEN IF YOU ARE AN EMPLOYEE.

(a) Were you self-employed this year and/or last year? ☐ Yes (If "Yes," answer (b),)

☐ No (If "No," go to item 22.)

(b) Check the year or years in which you were self-employed

☐ This Year

In what kind of trade or business were you self-employed? (For example, storekeeper, farmer, physician.) _____

Were your net earnings from your trade or business $400 or more? Check ☐ Yes ☐ No

☐ Last Year

In what kind of trade or business were you self-employed? (For example, storekeeper, farmer, physician.) _____

Were your net earnings from your trade or business $400 or more? Check ☐ Yes ☐ No

22. (a) How much were your total earnings last year? Amount $_____

(b) Place an "X" in each block for EACH MONTH of last year in which you did not earn more than *$_____ in wages, and did not perform substantial services in self-employment. These months are exempt months. If no months were exempt months, place an "X" in "NONE". If all months were exempt months, place an "X" in "ALL".

☐ NONE ☐ ALL

☐ Jan.   ☐ Feb.   ☐ Mar.   ☐ Apr.
☐ May   ☐ Jun.   ☐ July   ☐ Aug.
☐ Sept.   ☐ Oct.   ☐ Nov.   ☐ Dec.

*Enter the appropriate monthly limit after reading the instructions, "How Work Affects Your Benefits".

23. (a) How much do you expect your total earnings to be this year? Amount $_____

(b) Place an "X" in each block for EACH MONTH of this year in which you did not earn more than *$_____ in wages, and did not or will not perform substantial services in self-employment. These months are exempt months. If no months are or will be exempt months, place an "X" in "NONE". If all months are or will be exempt months, place an "X" in "ALL".

☐ NONE ☐ ALL

☐ Jan.   ☐ Feb.   ☐ Mar.   ☐ Apr.
☐ May   ☐ Jun.   ☐ July   ☐ Aug.
☐ Sept.   ☐ Oct.   ☐ Nov.   ☐ Dec.

*Enter the appropriate monthly limit after reading the instructions, "How Work Affects Your Benefits."

Answer this item ONLY if you are now in the last 4 months of your taxable year (Sept., Oct., Nov., and Dec., if your taxable year is a calendar year).

24. (a) How much do you expect to earn next year? Amount $_____
    (b) Place an "X" in each block for EACH MONTH of next year in which you do not expect to earn more than *$_____ in wages, and do not expect to perform substantial services in self-employment. These months will be exempt months. If no months are expected to be exempt months, place an "X" in "NONE". If all months are expected to be exempt months, place an "X" in "ALL".

    ☐ NONE ☐ ALL

☐ Jan.	☐ Feb.	☐ Mar.	☐ Apr.
☐ May	☐ Jun.	☐ July	☐ Aug.
☐ Sept.	☐ Oct.	☐ Nov.	☐ Dec.

*Enter the appropriate monthly limit after reading the instructions, "How Work Affects Your Benefits."

25. If you use a fiscal year, that is, a taxable year that does not end December 31 (with income tax return due April 15), enter here the month your fiscal year ends. Month _____

DO NOT ANSWER ITEM 26 IF YOU ARE FULL RETIREMENT AGE AND 6 MONTHS OR OLDER. YOU MAY HAVE MORE FILING OPTIONS; A SOCIAL SECURITY REPRESENTATIVE WILL CONTACT YOU TO DISCUSS ADDITIONAL INFORMATION THAT MAY HELP YOU DECIDE WHEN TO START YOUR BENEFIT. GO TO ITEM 27.

PLEASE READ CAREFULLY THE INFORMATION ON THE BOTTOM OF PAGE 57 AND ANSWER ONE OF THE FOLLOWING ITEMS:

26. (a) ☐ I want benefits beginning with the earliest possible month, and will accept an age-related reduction.
    (b) ☐ I am full retirement age (or will be within 12 months), and want benefits beginning with the earliest possible month providing there is no permanent reduction in my ongoing monthly benefits.
    (c) ☐ I want benefits beginning with _____

MEDICARE INFORMATION

If this claim is approved and you are still entitled to benefits at age 65, or you are within 3 months of age 65 or older you could automatically receive Medicare Part A (Hospital Insurance) and Medicare Part B (Medical Insurance) coverage at age 65. If you live in Puerto Rico or a foreign country, you are not eligible for automatic enrollment in Medicare Part B, and you will need to contact Social Security to request enrollment.

COMPLETE ITEM 27 ONLY IF YOU ARE WITHIN 3 MONTHS OF AGE 65 OR OLDER

Medicare Part B (Medical Insurance) helps cover doctor's services and outpatient care. It also covers some other services that Medicare Part A does not cover, such as some of the services of physical and occupational therapists and some home health care. If you enroll in Medicare Part B, you will have to pay a monthly premium. The amount of your premium will be determined when your coverage begins. In some cases, your premium may be higher based on information about your income we receive from the Internal Revenue Service. Your premiums will be deducted from any monthly Social Security, Railroad Retirement, or Office of Personnel Management benefits you receive. If you do not receive any of these benefits, you will get a letter explaining how to pay your premiums. You will also get a letter if there is any change in the amount of your premium.

You can also enroll in a Medicare prescription drug plan (Part D). To learn more about the Medicare prescription drug plans and when you can enroll, visit www.medicare.gov or call 1-800-MEDICARE (1-800-633-4227; TTY 1-877-486-2048). Medicare can also tell you about agencies in your area that can help you choose your prescription drug coverage. The amount of your premium varies based on the prescription drug plan provider. The amount you pay for Part D coverage may be higher than the listed plan premium, based on information about your income we receive from the Internal Revenue Service.

If you have limited income and resources, we encourage you to apply for the Extra Help that is available to assist you with Medicare prescription drug costs. The Extra Help can pay the monthly premiums, annual deductibles, and prescription co-payments. To learn more or apply, please visit www.socialsecurity.gov, call 1-800-772-1213 (TTY 1-800-325-0778) or visit the nearest Social Security office.

27. Do you want to enroll in Medicare Part B (Medical Insurance)? ☐ Yes ☐ No

28. If you are within 2 months of age 65 or older, blind or disabled, do you want to file for Supplemental Security Income? ☐ Yes ☐ No

REMARKS (You may us this space for any explanations. If you need more space, attach a separate sheet.)

_____

_____

_____

I declare under penalty of perjury that I have examined all the information on this form, and on any accompanying statements or forms, and it is true and correct to the best of my knowledge. I understand that anyone who knowingly gives a false statement about a material fact in this information, or causes someone else to do so, commits a crime and may be subject to a fine or imprisonment.

SIGNATURE OF APPLICANT

SIGNATURE (First Name, Middle Initial, Last Name) (Write in ink.)
Date (Month, day, year)_____
Telephone number(s) at which you may be contacted during the day_____

DIRECT DEPOSIT PAYMENT INFORMATION (Financial Institution)
Routing Transit Number_____
Account Number_____
☐ Checking
☐ Savings

☐ Enroll in Direct Deposit
☐ Direct Deposit Refused

Applicant's Mailing Address (Number and street, Apt. No., P.O. Box, or Rural Route)
(Enter Residence Address in "Remarks," if different.) _____
City and State_____ ZIP Code_____
County (if any) in which you now live_____

Witnesses are required ONLY if this application has been signed by mark (X) above. If you signed by mark (X), two witnesses who know the applicant must sign below, giving their full addresses. Also, print the applicant's name in the Signature block.

1. Signature of Witness_____

   Address (Number and Street, City, State and ZIP Code) _____

   _____

2. Signature of Witness_____

   Address (Number and Street, City, State and ZIP Code) _____

   _____

Privacy Act Statement
Collection and Use of Information

Sections 202, 205, 223 and 1872 of the Social Security Act, as amended, allow us to collect this information. Furnishing us this information is voluntary. However, failing to provide all or part of the information may prevent an accurate and timely decision on any claim filed.

We will use the information to make a determination of eligibility for benefits for you and your dependents. We may also share your information for the following purposes, called routine uses:

1. To the Office of Personnel Management (OPM) the fact that a veteran is, or is not, eligible for retirement insurance benefits under the Social Security program for OPM's use in determining a veteran's eligibility for a civil service retirement annuity and the amount of such annuity; and
2. To the Department of State and its agents for administering the Social Security Act in foreign countries through facilities and services to that agency.

In addition, we may share this information in accordance with the Privacy Act and other Federal laws. For example, where authorized, we may use and disclose this information in computer matching programs, in which our records are compared with other records to establish or verify a person's eligibility for Federal benefit programs and for repayment of incorrect or delinquent debts under these programs.

A list of additional routine uses is available in our Privacy Act System of Records Notices (SORNs) 60-0059, entitled Earnings Recording and Self-Employment Income System and 60-0089, entitled Claims Folders Systems. Additional information and a full listing of our SORNs are available on our website at www.socialsecurity.gov/foia/bluebook.

CHANGES TO BE REPORTED AND HOW TO REPORT

Failure to report may result in overpayments that must be repaid, and in possible monetary penalties

- You change your mailing address for checks or residence. (To avoid delay in receipt of checks you should ALSO file a regular change of address notice with your post office.)
- Your citizenship or immigration status changes.
- You go outside the U.S.A. for 30 consecutive days or longer.
- Any beneficiary dies or becomes unable to handle benefits.
- Work Changes – On your application you told us you expect total earnings for _____ (year) to be
  $_____.
  You ☐ (are) ☐ (are not) earning wages of more than $_____ a month.
  You ☐ (are) ☐ (are not) self-employed rendering substantial services in your trade or business.
  (Report AT ONCE if this work pattern changes.)
- You are confined to a jail, prison, penal institution or correctional facility for more than 30 continuous days for conviction of a crime, or you are confined for more than 30 continuous days to a public institution by a court order in connection with a crime.
- You have an unsatisfied warrant for more than 30 continuous days for your arrest for a crime or attempted crime that is a felony of flight to avoid prosecution or confinement, escape from custody and flight-escape. In most jurisdictions that do not classify crimes as felonies, this applies to a crime that is punishable by death or imprisonment for a term exceeding one year (regardless of the actual sentence imposed).
- You have an unsatisfied warrant for more than 30 continuous days for a violation of probation or parole under Federal or State law.
- You become entitled to a pension, an annuity, or a lump sum payment based on your employment not covered by Social Security, or if such pension or annuity stops.
- Your stepchild is entitled to benefits on your record and you and the stepchild's parent divorce. Stepchild benefits are not payable beginning with the month after the month the divorce becomes final.

- Custody Change – Report if a person for whom you are filing or who is in your care dies, leaves your care or custody, or changes address.
- Change of Marital Status – Marriage, divorce, annulment of marriage.
- If you become the parent of a child (including an adopted child) after you have filed your claim, let us know about the child so we can decide if the child is eligible for benefits. Failure to report the existence of these children may result in the loss of possible benefits to the child(ren).

HOW TO REPORT

You can make your reports online, by telephone, mail, or in person, whichever you prefer.

If you are awarded benefits, and one or more of the above change(s) occur, you should report by:

- Visiting the section "mySocialSecurity" at our web site at www.socialsecurity.gov.
- Calling us TOLL FREE at 1-800-772-1213.
- If you are deaf or hearing impaired, calling us TOLL FREE at 1-800-325-0778; or
- Calling, visiting or writing your local Social Security office at the phone number and address shown on your claim receipt.

For general information about Social Security, visit our web site at www.socialsecurity.gov.

For those under full retirement age, the law requires that a report of earnings be filed with SSA within 3 months and 15 days after the end of any taxable year in which you earn more than the annual exempt amount. You may contact SSA to file a report. Otherwise, SSA will use the earnings reported by your employer(s) and your self-employment tax return (if applicable) as the report of earnings required by law, to adjust benefits under the earnings test. It is your responsibility to ensure that the information you give concerning your earnings is correct. You must furnish additional information as needed when your benefit adjustment is not correct based on the earnings on your record.

PLEASE READ THE FOLLOWING INFORMTION CAREFULLY BEFORE YOU ANSWER QUESTION 26.

- If you are under full retirement age, retirement benefits cannot be payable to you for any month before the month in which you file your claim.
- If you are over full retirement age, retirement benefits may be payable to you for some months before the month in which you file this claim.
- If your first month of entitlement is prior to full retirement age, your benefit rate will be reduced. However, if you do not actually receive your full benefit amount for one or more months before full retirement age because benefits are withheld due to your earnings, your benefit will be increased at the full retirement age to give credit for this withholding. Thus, your benefit amount at full retirement age will be reduced only if you receive one or more full benefit payments prior to the month you attain full retirement age.

•• Delayed retirement credits may be added to your benefits if you request them to start when you are full retirement age or older.

•• Please visit our www.ssa.gov web site to use the Retirement Estimator to get a personal estimate of how much your benefits will be at different ages. In addition, our web site provides information about other things you should think about when you make your decision about when to begin your benefits.

Chapter Six

Spouses, Dependents, and Survivors

[EDITOR'S NOTE: See also Chapter 8 for "Recent Changes in Deemed Filing," and "File and Suspend."]

40. What are five things every woman should know about Social Security?

41. What is the eligibility for Social Security spouse's benefits and my own retirement benefits?

42. When can my spouse get Social Security benefits on my record?

43. What are the marriage requirements to receive Social Security spouse's benefits?

44. Can I get Social Security benefits on my former spouse's record?

45. Can my former spouse get benefits on my Social Security record?

46. How much can a divorced spouse receive?

47. Do I qualify for benefits as a spouse if I am now in, or the surviving spouse of, a civil union, domestic partnership, or other non-marital legal relationship?

48. I am receiving Social Security benefits. Must I tell Social Security if I am in a civil union or other non-marital legal relationship?

49. Can children and students get Social Security benefits?

50. Can children with disabilities get Social Security benefits?

51. Who can get parent's benefits?

52. Who can get Social Security survivors benefits and how do I apply?

53. Is there a limit to the amount of monthly benefits my family can get on my record?

54. Who can get a lump-sum death benefit?

55. What does the Application for Wife's or Husband's Insurance Benefits look like?

40. What are the five things every woman should know about Social Security?

For more than 80 years, Social Security has helped secure today and tomorrow by providing benefits and financial protection for millions of people throughout their life's journey. Here are the five most important things every woman should know about Social Security.

1. Nothing keeps you from getting your own Social Security benefit.

- If you've worked and paid taxes into the Social Security system for at least 10 years and have earned a minimum of 40 work credits, you may be eligible for your own benefits.
- Once you reach age 62, you may be eligible for your own Social Security benefit whether you're married or not and whether your spouse collects Social Security or not.
- We figure everyone's retirement benefit the same way. It's based on a percentage of your average monthly wage using a 35-year base of earnings. If you don't have 35 years of earnings, we must substitute "zero" years to reach the 35-year base.
- If you become disabled before your full retirement age, you might qualify for Social Security disability benefits, if you worked and paid Social Security taxes in five of the last 10 years.
- If you also get a pension from a job where you didn't pay Social Security taxes (e.g., a civil service or teacher's pension), your Social Security benefit might be reduced.

2. There is no marriage penalty or limit to benefits paid a married couple.

- If you are married and you and your spouse have worked and earned enough credits individually, you will each get your own Social Security benefit.

- A working woman is not limited to one-half of her spouse's Social Security. (That rate applies to women who never worked outside the home.)
- So, for example, if you are due a Social Security benefit of $1,200 per month and your spouse is due a Social Security benefit of $1,400 per month, the two of you will get $2,600 per month in retirement benefits.

3. If you're due two benefits, you get the one that pays the higher rate, not both.

- As a spouse, you are potentially eligible for benefits on both your own and your spouse's work record, but you only receive the one that pays the higher rate, not both.
- A wife is eligible for between one-third and one-half of her spouse's Social Security benefit, if she does not have her own work record.
- Most working women who reach retirement age receive their own Social Security benefit amount because it's more than one-third to one-half of their spouse's rate.
- If your spouse dies before you, you can apply for the higher widow's rate. (See #5 in this list.)

4. If you're divorced and were married at least 10 years, you're eligible on your ex's Social Security record.

- Divorced women who were married at least 10 years are eligible for Social Security based on their ex's record, if they are unmarried when they become eligible for Social Security.
- Some women sign divorce decrees relinquishing their rights to Social Security on their ex's record. Those clauses in divorce decrees are never enforced.

- Any benefits paid to a divorced spouse DO NOT reduce payments made to the ex or any payments due the ex's current spouse.
- Generally, the same payment rules apply to divorced wives and widows as to current wives and widows. That means most divorced women collect their own Social Security while the ex is alive, but they can apply for higher widow's rates when they die.

5. When your spouse (or ex) dies, you're probably due a widow's benefit.

- A widow is eligible for between 71 percent (at age 60) and 100 percent (at full retirement age) of what the spouse was getting before they died.
- We must pay your own retirement benefit first, then supplement it with whatever extra benefits you are due as a widow, to bring your Social Security benefit amount up to the widow's rate.
- We also can pay you a $255 one-time death benefit if you were living with your spouse when they died.
- If you made more money than your spouse, then they [your spouse and exes] might be due a survivors benefit rate on your record, if you die before they do.

Learn more by reading our publication *What Every Woman Should Know* at www.socialsecurity.gov/pubs/EN-05-10127.pdf.

41. What is the eligibility for Social Security spouse's benefits and my own retirement benefits?

If you have not worked or do not have enough Social Security credits to qualify for your own Social Security benefits, you may be able to receive spouse's benefits.

To qualify for spouse's benefits, you must be:

- At least 62 years of age; or
- Any age and caring for a child entitled to receive benefits on your spouse's record who is younger than age 16 or disabled.

Your full spouse's benefit could be up to one-half the amount your spouse is entitled to receive at their full retirement age. If you choose to begin receiving spouse's benefits before you reach full retirement age, your benefit amount will be permanently reduced.

You will receive your full spouse's benefit amount if you wait until you reach full retirement age to begin receiving benefits. You will also receive the full amount if you are caring for a child entitled to receive benefits on your spouse's record who is younger than age 16 or disabled.

If you do have enough credits to qualify for your own Social Security benefits and you apply for your own retirement benefits and for benefits as a spouse, we always pay your own benefits first. If your benefits as a spouse are higher than your own retirement benefits, you will get a combination of benefits equaling the higher spouse benefit.

42. When can my spouse get Social Security benefits on my record?

Your spouse may be able to get benefits if he or she is at least age 62 and you are getting, or are eligible for, retirement or disability benefits. We also will pay benefits to your spouse at any age if there is a child in his or her care. The child must be under age 16 or disabled before age 22, and entitled to benefits. Your spouse also can qualify for Medicare at age 65.

43. What are the marriage requirements to receive Social Security spouse's benefits?

Generally, you must be married for one year before you can get spouse's benefits. However, if you are the parent of your spouse's child, the one-year rule does not apply. The same is true if you were entitled (or potentially entitled) to certain benefits under Social Security or the Railroad Retirement Act in the month before the month you got married. A divorced spouse must have been married 10 years to get spouse's benefits.

44. Can I get Social Security benefits on my former spouse's record?

If you are divorced and your marriage lasted at least 10 years, you may be able to get benefits on your former spouse's record.

45. Can my former spouse get benefits on my Social Security record?

If you are divorced and your marriage lasted at least 10 years, your former spouse may be able to get benefits based on your record.

46. How much can a divorced spouse receive?

The maximum benefit a divorced spouse can receive is 50 percent of the benefit the worker would receive at full retirement age. However, benefits paid before the full retirement age of the spouse are reduced based upon the age of the spouse at the time benefits are received.

See the chart below for the reduction in benefits.

			At Age 62[3]			
Year of Birth[1]	Full (normal) Retirement Age	Months between age 62 and full retirement age[2]	A $1000 retirement benefit would be reduced to	The retirement benefit is reduced by[4]	A $500 spouse's benefit would be reduced to	The spouse's benefit is reduced by[5]
Full Retirement and Age 62 Benefit by Year of Birth						
1937 or earlier	65	36	$800	20.00%	$375	25.00%
1938	65 and 2 months	38	$791	20.83%	$370	25.83%
1939	65 and 4 months	40	$783	21.67%	$366	26.67%
1940	65 and 6 months	42	$775	22.50%	$362	27.50%
1941	65 and 8 months	44	$766	23.33%	$358	28.33%
1942	65 and 10 months	46	$758	24.17%	$354	29.17%
1943-1954	66	48	$750	25.00%	$350	30.00%
1955	66 and 2 months	50	$741	25.83%	$345	30.83%
1956	66 and 4 months	52	$733	26.67%	$341	31.67%
1957	66 and 6 months	54	$725	27.50%	$337	32.50%
1958	66 and 8 months	56	$716	28.33%	$333	33.33%
1959	66 and 10 months	58	$708	29.17%	$329	34.17%
1960 and later	67	60	$700	30.00%	$325	35.00%

[1] If you were born on January 1st, you should refer to the previous year.
[2] If you were born on the 1st of the month, we figure your benefit (and your full retirement age) as if your birthday was in the previous month. If you were born on January 1st, we figure your benefit (and your full retirement age) as if your birthday was in December of the previous year.
[3] You must be at least 62 for the entire month to receive benefits.
[4] Percentages are approximate due to rounding.
[5] The maximum benefit for the spouse is 50% of the benefit the worker would receive at full retirement age. The % reduction for the spouse should be applied after the automatic 50% reduction. Percentages are approximate due to rounding.

47. Do I qualify for benefits as a spouse if I am now in, or the surviving spouse of, a civil union, domestic partnership, or other non-marital legal relationship?

Social Security is now processing some retirement, surviving spouse and lump-sum death payment claims for same-sex couples in non-marital legal relationships (such as some civil unions and domestic partnerships) and paying benefits where they are due. We encourage you to apply right away for benefits, even if you aren't sure you are eligible. Applying now will protect you against the loss of any potential benefits.

If you have questions about how a same-sex marriage may affect your claim, please call 1-800-772-1213 (TTY 1-800-325-0778) or contact your local Social Security office.

48. I am receiving Social Security benefits. Must I tell Social Security I am in a civil union or other non-marital legal relationship?

Your status in a civil union or other non-marital legal relationship may affect your entitlement to benefits. You must tell us if you are in a civil union or other non-marital legal relationship.

If you have questions about how a same-sex civil union or non-marital legal relationship may affect your claim, please call 1-800-772-1213 (TTY 1-800-325-0778) or contact your local Social Security office.

49. Can children and students get Social Security benefits?

When a parent gets Social Security retirement benefits or disability benefits, his or her child also may get benefits. Children also can get benefits when a parent dies. The child can be a biological child, adopted child or stepchild. A dependent grandchild also may qualify.

To get benefits, the child must be unmarried and:

- Younger than age 18;
- A full-time student (no higher than grade 12) 18 to 19 years old; or
- Have a disability that started before age 22 and is 18 years or older.

50. Can children with disabilities get Social Security benefits?

A child with a disability age 18 or older may get Social Security benefits when a parent gets retirement or disability benefits. The child can also get benefits if a parent dies. The child's disability must have begun before age 22.

51. Who can get parent's benefits?

When a worker dies, Social Security benefits help to stabilize the family's financial future. Survivors benefits provide financial support to eligible individuals who depended on the worker's income before the worker's death. Along with the worker's children and spouses, the dependent parents also may be eligible for a survivors benefit.

For a parent to be eligible for a benefit, the following must be true:

- The parent is at least 62;
- The parent was receiving at least one-half of their support from the deceased worker at the time of death (or at the beginning of the deceased worker's disability);
- The parent has provided timely documents that prove the deceased worker was providing at least one-half of their support;
- The parent is not entitled to a retirement insurance benefit equal to or exceeding the parent's new benefit;

- The parent is the natural parent of the deceased worker (or became the stepparent or adoptive parent before the deceased worker reached the age of 16);
- The parent has not married after the worker's death; and
- The deceased worker had enough work credits.

How Much a Parent Can Get.

One parent may receive 82½ percent of the deceased worker's full retirement or disability benefit. If there are two parents who will receive benefits, each may receive 75 percent.

What a Parent Who Receives Benefits Needs to Know.

- The parent's benefit may stop if the parent marries.
- The parent's benefit will stop if the parent becomes entitled to a retirement benefit amount higher than the parent's benefit amount.

---

52. Who can get Social Security survivors benefits and how do I apply?

When you die, members of your family could be eligible for benefits based on your earnings. You and your children also may be able to get benefits if your deceased spouse or former spouse worked long enough under Social Security.

Who Can Get Survivors Benefits.

Widows and Widowers
A widow or widower can receive benefits:
- at age 60 or older.
- at age 50 or older if disabled.

- at any age if she or he takes care of a child of the deceased who is younger than age 16 or disabled.

Divorced Widows and Widowers
A divorced widow or widower can receive benefits:
- at age 60 or older if the marriage to the deceased lasted at least 10 years.
- at age 50 or older if disabled and the marriage to the deceased lasted at least 10 years.
- at any age if she or he takes care of a child of the deceased who is younger than age 16 or disabled.

Unmarried Children
Unmarried children can receive benefits if they are:
- younger than age 18 (or up to age 19 if they are attending elementary or secondary school full time).
- any age and were disabled before age 22 and remain disabled. (Under certain circumstances, benefits also can be paid to stepchildren, grandchildren, step-grandchildren, or adopted children.)

Dependent Parents
Parents age 62 or older who received at least one-half support from the deceased can receive benefits.

One-time Lump Sum Death Payment
A one-time payment of $255 can be made only to a spouse or child if they meet certain requirements. Survivors must apply for this payment within two years of the date of death.

How to Apply for Survivors Benefits

You cannot apply for survivors benefits online. To report a death or apply for survivors benefits, please call our toll-free number, 1-800-772-1213 (TTY 1-800-325-0778).

You also can call or visit your local Social Security office.

53. Is there a limit to the amount of monthly benefits my family can get on my record?

There is a limit to the amount we can pay your family. The total depends on your benefit amount and the number of family members who also qualify on your record. The total varies, but generally, the total amount you and your family can get is about 150 to 180 percent of your full retirement benefit.

The benefit payments we make to a divorced spouse do not affect the benefits payable to you or any other family member.

54. Who can get a lump-sum death benefit?

We may pay a lump-sum death benefit of $255 to:

- A spouse who was living with the deceased person at the time of death; or
- A spouse or a child who, in the month of death, is eligible for a Social Security benefit based on the deceased person's record.

Information You Need to Apply for Lump Sum Death Benefit—
Form SSA-8.

You can apply for benefits by calling our national toll-free service at 1-800-772-1213 (TTY 1-800-325-0778) or by visiting your local Social Security office. An appointment is not required, but if you call ahead and schedule one, it may reduce the time you spend waiting to apply.

You can help by being ready to:

- Provide any needed documents; and
- Answer the questions listed below.

Documents You May Need to Provide.

We may ask you to provide documents to show that you are eligible, such as:

- A birth certificate or other proof of birth;
- Proof of U.S. citizenship or lawful alien status if you were not born in the United States; [see Chapter Five, question #38 for acceptable documents]
- U.S. military discharge paper(s) if you had military service before 1968;
- W-2 forms(s) and/or self-employment tax returns for last year; and
- A death certificate for the deceased worker.

NOTE: We accept photocopies of W-2 forms or self-employment tax returns, but we must see the original of most other documents, such as your birth certificate. We will return the documents to you.

Do not delay applying for benefits because you do not have all the documents. We will help you get them.

IF YOU NEED TO SHOW ORIGINAL DOCUMENTS: We must see the original document(s) or copies certified by the agency that issued them. We cannot accept photocopies or notarized copies. We will return all your documents to you unless you specifically tell us otherwise. If you have the documents we need, you should submit them as soon as possible. If you don't have all the documents, you should submit any documents you do have. We will help you get the other documents.

IMPORTANT: If you mail any documents to us, we must have your Social Security Number so we can match them with your application. Please write your Social Security Number on a separate sheet of paper and include it in the mailing envelope along with your documents.

DO NOT write anything on your original documents. If you do not want to mail your documents, you may bring them to the Social Security office where we will examine and return them to you. Or, if a later office visit becomes necessary, you may bring them with you at that time.

CAUTION: Do not mail foreign birth records or any Department of Homeland Security (DHS) documents to us—especially those you are required to keep with you at all times. These documents are extremely difficult, time-consuming, and expensive to replace if lost. Some cannot be replaced. Instead, bring them to the Social Security office where we will examine and return them to you.

What We Will Ask You For.

- Your name and Social Security number;
- The deceased worker's name, gender, date of birth, and Social Security number;
- The deceased worker's date and place of death;
- Whether the deceased worker ever filed for Social Security benefits, Medicare, or Supplemental Security Income (if so, we will also ask for information on whose Social Security record he or she applied);

- Whether the deceased worker was unable to work because of illnesses, injuries, or conditions at any time during the 14 months before his or her death (if "Yes," we will also ask when he or she became unable to work);
- Whether the deceased worker was ever in the active military service (if "Yes," we will also ask for the dates of his or her service);
- Whether the deceased worker worked for the railroad industry for 7 years or more;
- Whether the deceased worker earned Social Security credits under another country's social security system;
- The names, dates of birth (or age), and Social Security numbers (if known) of any of the deceased worker's former spouses and the dates of the marriages and how and when they ended;
- The names of any of the deceased worker's unmarried children under 18, 18–19 and in secondary school, or disabled prior to age 22;
- The amount of the deceased worker's earnings in the year of death and the preceding year;
- Whether the deceased worker had a parent who was dependent on the worker for one-half of his or her support at the time of the worker's death; and
- Whether the deceased worker and surviving spouse were living together at the time of death.

If you are the surviving spouse, we will also ask:

- Whether you have been unable to work because of illnesses, injuries, or conditions at any time within the past 14 months (if "Yes," we will also ask when you became unable to work);
- Whether you or anyone else ever filed for Social Security benefits, Medicare, or Supplemental Security Income on your behalf (if so, we will also ask for information on whose Social Security record you applied); and

- The names, dates of birth (or age), and social security numbers (if known) of any of your former spouses and the dates of the marriages and how and when they ended.

If you are not the surviving spouse, we will also ask for the surviving spouse's name and address.

NOTE: You also should have with you your checkbook or other papers that show your account number at a bank, credit union, or other financial institution so you can sign up for Direct Deposit, and avoid worries about lost or stolen checks and mail delays.

55. What does the Application for Wife's or Husband's Insurance Benefits look like?

SAMPLE ONLY—DO NOT USE FOR SUBMISSION!

Form SSA-2-BK (03-2017) UF (3-2017)

APPLICATION FOR WIFE'S OR HUSBAND'S INSURANCE BENEFITS

I apply for all insurance benefits for which I am eligible under Title II (Federal Old-Age, Survivors, and Disability Insurance) and Part A of Title XVIII (Health Insurance for the Aged and Disabled) of the Social Security Act, as presently amended.

☐ Supplement, if you have already completed an application entitled "APPLICATION FOR RETIREMENT INSURANCE BENEFITS", you need complete only the circled items. All other claimants must complete the entire form.

①(a) PRINT Name of Wage Earner or Self-Employed Person (Herein referred to as the "Worker")
   FIRST NAME, MIDDLE INITIAL, LAST NAME _____
   (b) Enter Worker's Social Security Number_____

2. Check (X) whether you are ☐ Male   ☐ Female

③.ⓐ PRINT your name: FIRST NAME, MIDDLE INITIAL, LAST NAME_____

_____

ⓑ Enter your Social Security Number_____

Answer question 4 if English is not your preferred language. Otherwise, go to item 5.

4. Enter the language you prefer to: Speak _____ Write _____

5.(a) Enter your date of birth: MONTH, DAY, YEAR _____
   (b) Enter name of city and state, or foreign country where you were born. _____
   (c) Was a public record of your birth made before you were age 5? ☐ Yes ☐ No ☐ Unknown
   (d) Was a religious record of your birth made before you were age 5? ☐ Yes ☐ No ☐ Unknown

6. (a) Are you a U.S. citizen? ☐ Yes (If "Yes," go to item 7.) ☐ No (If "No," answer (b).)
   (b) Are you an alien lawfully present in the U.S.? ☐ Yes (Go to item (c).) ☐ No (Go to item 7.)
   (c) When were you lawfully admitted to the U.S.? _____

7. (a)Enter your full name at birth if different from item 3(a). FIRST NAME, MIDDLE INITIAL,
   LAST NAME _____
   (b) Have you used any other name(s)? ☐ Yes (If "Yes," go answer (c).) ☐ No (Go to item 8.)
   (c) Other name(s) used _____

8.(a) Have you used any other Social Security number(s)? ☐ Yes ☐ No
   (b) Enter Social Security number(s) used. _____

Do not answer question 9 if you are one year past full retirement age or older; go on to question 10.

⑨.(a) Are you, or during the past 14 months have you been, unable to work because of illnesses,
   injuries, or conditions? ☐ Yes (If "Yes," answer (b).) ☐ No (If "No," go to item 10.)
   (b) If "Yes" when do you believe your condition(s) became severe enough to keep you from working
   (even if you have never worked)? MONTH, DAY, YEAR_____

10. (a) Have you (or has someone on your behalf) ever filed an application for Social Security benefits,
    a period of disability under Social Security, Supplemental Security Income, or hospital or medical
    insurance under Medicare? ☐ Yes (If "Yes," answer (b) and (c).) ☐ No (If "No," go to item 11.)

10. (b) Enter the name of the person(s) on whose Social Security record you filed other application.
FIRST NAME, MIDDLE INITIAL, LAST NAME _____

(c) Enter Social Security Number(s) of person named in (b). (If unknown, so indicate.)

_____

11. (a) Were you in the active military or naval service (including Reserve or National Guard active duty or active duty for training) after September 7, 1939 and before 1968?
☐ Yes (If "Yes," answer (b) and (c).) ☐ No (If "No," go to item 12.) (b) Enter date(s) of service:
From (Month, Year) _____ To (Month, Year) _____
(c) Have you ever been (or will you be) eligible for monthly benefits from a military or civilian Federal agency (Include Veterans Administration benefits only if you waived Military retirement pay)? ☐ Yes ☐ No

12. Did you, or your spouse, (or prior spouse) work in the railroad industry for 5 years or more?
☐ Yes ☐ No

13. (a) Do you have Social Security credits (for example, based on work or residence) under another country's Social Security system? ☐ Yes (If "Yes," answer (b).) ☐ No (If "No," go to item 14.)
(b) List the country(ies): _____

14. (a) Are you entitled to, or do you expect to be entitled to, a pension or annuity (or a lump sum in place of a pension or annuity) based on your own employment and earnings from the Federal government of the United States, or one of its States or local subdivisions? (Social Security benefits are not government pensions.)
☐ Yes (If "Yes," check which of the items in.item (b) applies to you.)
☐ No (If "No," go on to item 15.)
(b) Check one box and provide the date in (c).
☐ I receive a government pension or annuity.
☐ I received a lump sum in place of a government pension or annuity.
☐ I applied for and am awaiting a decision on my pension or lump sum.
☐ I have not applied for but I expect to begin receiving my pension or annuity.
(c) MONTH/ YEAR_____(If the date is not known, enter "Unknown.")

I agree to promptly notify the Social Security Administration if I become entitled to a pension, an annuity, or a lump sum payment based on my employment not covered by Social Security, or if my pension or annuity amount changes or stops.

15. (a) Enter information about your marriage to the worker. If you married the worker more than once, use the "Remarks" space to enter the additional marriage information. Go to item 15(b) if you are filing as a divorced spouse; otherwise, go to item 15 (c).

Spouse's name (including maiden name): _____

When (Month, day, year)_____

Where (Name of City and State)_____

How marriage ended (if still in effect, write "Not Ended.") _____

When (Month, day, year) _____

Where (Name of City and State) _____

Marriage performed by

☐ Clergyman or public official

☐ Other (Explain in "Remarks")

Spouse's date of birth (or age) _____

If spouse deceased, give date of death _____

Spouse's Social Security number (if none or unknown, so indicate) _____

(b) If you remarried after the divorce from the worker, enter the marriage information. If you did not remarry, write "None." Go on to item 15(c) if you had other marriages.

Spouse's name (including maiden name): _____

When (Month, day, year)_____

Where (Name of City and State)_____

How marriage ended (if still in effect, write "Not Ended.") _____

When (Month, day, year) _____

Where (Name of City and State) _____

Marriage performed by

☐ Clergyman or public official

☐ Other (Explain in "Remarks")

Spouse's date of birth (or age) _____

If spouse deceased, give date of death _____

Spouse's Social Security number (if none or unknown, so indicate) _____

(c) Enter information about any marriage if you:

• Had a marriage that lasted at least 10 years; or

• Had a marriage that ended due to the death of your spouse, regardless of duration; or

• Were divorced, remarried the same individual within the year immediately following the year of the divorce, and the combined period of the marriage totaled 10 years or more. Use the "Remarks" space to enter the additional marriage information. Do not repeat any marriages listed in item 15(a) or 15(b). If None, write "None."_____

To whom married _____

When (Month, day, year) _____

Where (Name of City and State)_____

How marriage ended (if still in effect, write "Not Ended.") _____

When (Month, day, year) _____

Where (Name of City and State) _____

Marriage performed by

☐ Clergyman or public official

☐ Other (Explain in "Remarks")

Spouse's date of birth (or age) _____

If spouse deceased, give date of death _____

Spouse's Social Security number (if none or unknown, so indicate) _____

(Use "Remarks" space on page 83 for information about any other marriages.)

If you are now under full retirement age or less than one year past full retirement age, answer question 16. If you are more than one year past full retirement age, go to question 17.

16. Has an unmarried child of the worker (including adopted child, or stepchild) or a dependent grandchild of the worker (including step-grandchild) who is under 16 or disabled lived with you during any of the last 13 months (counting the present month)? (☐ Yes (If "Yes," enter the information requested below.) ☐ No

Name of child_____

Months child lived with you (if all, write "All")_____

Name of child_____

Months child lived with you (if all, write "All")_____

Name of child_____

Months child lived with you (if all, write "All")_____

17. Enter below the names and addresses of all the persons, companies, or government agencies for whom you have worked this year, last year, and the year before last. IF NONE, WRITE "NONE" BELOW AND GO ON TO ITEM 21.

NAME AND ADDRESS OF EMPLOYER (If you had more than one employer, please list them in order beginning with your last (most recent) employer.)

_____Work Began (Month/Year)_____

Work Ended (If still working, show "Not Ended") _____

_____Work Began (Month/Year)_____

Work Ended (If still working, show "Not Ended") _____

_____Work Began (Month/Year)_____

Work Ended (If still working, show "Not Ended") _____

_____Work Began (Month/Year)_____

Work Ended (If still working, show "Not Ended") _____

(If you need more space, use "Remarks".)

18. (a) How much were your total earnings last year? Amount $_____
    (b) Place an "X" in each block for EACH MONTH of last year in which you did not earn more than *$_____ in wages, and did not perform substantial services in self-employment. These months are exempt months. If no months were exempt months, place an "X" in "NONE". If all months were exempt months, place an "X" in "ALL".

☐ NONE ☐ ALL

☐ Jan.   ☐ Feb.   ☐ Mar.   ☐ Apr.
☐ May   ☐ Jun.   ☐ July   ☐ Aug.
☐ Sept. ☐ Oct.   ☐ Nov.   ☐ Dec.

*Enter the appropriate monthly limit after reading the instructions "How Work Affects Your Benefits".

19. (a) How much do you expect your total earnings to be this year? Amount $_____

(b) Place an "X" in each block for EACH MONTH of this year in which you did not or will not earn more than *$_____ in wages, and did not or will not perform substantial services in self-employment. These months are exempt months. If no months are or will be exempt months, place an "X" in "NONE". If all months are or will be exempt months, place an "X" in "ALL".

☐ NONE ☐ ALL

☐ Jan.	☐ Feb.	☐ Mar.	☐ Apr.
☐ May	☐ Jun.	☐ July	☐ Aug.
☐ Sept.	☐ Oct.	☐ Nov.	☐ Dec.

*Enter the appropriate monthly limit after reading the instructions "How Work Affects Your Benefits".

Answer this item ONLY if you are now in the last 4 months of your taxable year (Sept., Oct., Nov., and Dec., if your taxable year is a calendar year).

20. (a) How much do you expect to earn next year? Amount $_____

(b) Place an "X" in each block for EACH MONTH of next year in which you do not expect to earn more than *$_____ in wages, and do not expect to perform substantial services in self-employment. These months will be exempt months. If no months are expected to be exempt months, place an "X" in "NONE". If all months are expected to be exempt months, place an "X" in "ALL".

☐ NONE ☐ ALL

☐ Jan.	☐ Feb.	☐ Mar.	☐ Apr.
☐ May	☐ Jun.	☐ July	☐ Aug.
☐ Sept.	☐ Oct.	☐ Nov.	☐ Dec.

*Enter the appropriate monthly limit after reading the instructions "How Work Affects Your Benefits".

If you use a fiscal year, that is, a taxable year that does not end December 31 (with income tax return due April 15), enter here the month your fiscal year ends.
Month _____

If you are now under full retirement age and do not have an entitled child in your care, answer item 21. If you are full retirement age or older or you have an entitled child in your care, go to item 22.

PLEASE READ CAREFULLY THE INFORMATION ON THE BOTTOM OF PAGE 87 AND ANSWER ONE OF THE FOLLOWING ITEMS:

21. (a) I want benefits beginning with the earliest possible month, and will accept an age-related reduction. ☐

(b) I am full retirement age (or will be within 12 months), and want benefits beginning with the earliest possible month providing there is no permanent reduction in my ongoing monthly benefits. ☐

(c) I want benefits beginning with _____ ☐

MEDICARE INFORMATION

If this claim is approved and you are still entitled to benefits at age 65, or you are within 3 months of age 65 or older you could automatically receive Medicare Part A (Hospital Insurance) and Medicare Part B (Medical Insurance) coverage at age 65. If you live in Puerto Rico or a foreign country, you are not eligible for automatic enrollment in Medicare Part B, and you will need to contact Social Security to request enrollment.

COMPLETE ITEM 22 ONLY IF YOU ARE WITHIN 3 MONTHS OF AGE 65 OR OLDER

Medicare Part B (Medical Insurance) helps cover doctor's services and outpatient care. It also covers some other services that Medicare Part A does not cover, such as some of the services of physical and occupational therapists and some home health care. If you enroll in Medicare Part B, you will have to pay a monthly premium. The amount of your premium will be determined when your coverage begins. In some cases, your premium may be higher based on information about your income we receive from the Internal Revenue Service. Your premiums will be deducted from any monthly Social Security, Railroad Retirement, or Office of Personnel Management benefits you receive. If you do not receive any of these benefits, you will get a letter explaining how to pay your premiums. You will also get a letter if there is any change in the amount of your premium.

You can also enroll in a Medicare prescription drug plan (Part D). To learn more about the Medicare prescription drug plans and when you can enroll, visit www.medicare.gov or call 1-800-MEDICARE (1-800-633-4227; TTY 1-877-486-2048). Medicare can also tell you about agencies in your area that can help you choose your prescription drug coverage. The amount of your premium varies based on the prescription drug plan provider. The amount you pay for Part D coverage may be higher than the listed plan premium, based on information about your income we receive from the Internal Revenue Service.

If you have limited income and resources, we encourage you to apply for the Extra Help that is available to assist you with Medicare prescription drug costs. The Extra Help can pay the monthly premiums, annual deductibles, and prescription co-payments. To learn more or apply, please visit www.socialsecurity.gov, call 1-800-772-1213 (TTY 1-800-325-0778) or visit the nearest Social Security office.

22. Do you want to enroll in Medicare Part B (Medical Insurance)? ☐ Yes ☐ No

23. If you are within 2 months of age 65 or older, blind or disabled, do you want to file for Supplemental Security Income? ☐ Yes ☐ No

REMARKS (You may us this space for any explanations. If you need more space, attach a separate sheet.)

_____

_____

_____

I declare under penalty of perjury that I have examined all the information on this form, and on any accompanying statements or forms, and it is true and correct to the best of my knowledge. I understand that anyone who knowingly gives a false or misleading statement about a material fact in this information, or causes someone else to do so, commits a crime and may be sent to prison, or face other penalties, or both.

SIGNATURE OF APPLICANT

_____

SIGNATURE (First Name, Middle Initial, Last Name) (Write in ink.)
Date (Month, day, year)_____
Telephone number (s) at which you may be contacted during the day_____

DIRECT DEPOSIT PAYMENT INFORMATION (Financial Institution)
Routing Transit Number_____
Account Number_____
☐ Checking
☐ Savings
☐ Enroll in Direct Express
☐ Direct Deposit Refused

Applicant's Mailing Address (Number and street, Apt. No., P.O. Box, or Rural Route)
(Enter Residence Address in "Remarks," if different.) _____
City and State_____ ZIP Code_____
County (if any) in which you now live_____

Witnesses are required ONLY if this application has been signed by mark (X) above. If you signed by mark (X), two witnesses who know the applicant must sign below, giving their full addresses. Also, print the applicant's name in the Signature block.

1. Signature of Witness_____
   Address (Number and Street, City, State and ZIP Code)_____

2. Signature of Witness_____
   Address (Number and Street, City, State and ZIP Code)_____

Collection and Use of Information From Your Application – Privacy Act Notice/ Paperwork Reduction Act Notice. Sections 202, 205, 223 and 1872 of the Social Security Act, as amended, allow us to collect this information. Furnishing us this information is voluntary. However, failing to provide all or part of the information may prevent an accurate and timely decision on any claim filed.

We will use the information to make a determination of eligibility for benefits for you and your dependents. We may also share your information for the following purposes, called routine uses:

1. To any source that has, or is expected to have, information that the Social Security Administration (SSA) needs in order to establish or verify a person's eligibility for a certificate of coverage under a Social Security agreement authorized by section 233 of the Social Security Act (Act); and
2. To private medical and vocational consultants for use in making preparation for, or evaluation of the results of, consultative medical examinations or vocational assessments which they were engaged to perform by SSA or a State agency acting in accord with sections 221 or 1633 of the Act.

In addition, we may share this information in accordance with the Privacy Act and other Federal laws. For example, where authorized, we may use and disclose this information in computer matching programs, in which our records are compared with other records to establish or verify a person's eligibility for Federal benefit programs and for repayment of incorrect or delinquent debts under these programs.

A list of additional routine uses is available in our Privacy Act System of Records Notices (SORNs) 60-0059, entitled Earnings Recording and Self-Employment Income System and 60-0089, entitled Claims Folders Systems. Additional information and a full listing of our SORNs are available on our website at www.socialsecurity.gov/foia/bluebook.

Paperwork Reduction Act Statement – This information collection meets the requirements of 44 U.S.C. 3507, as amended by section 2 of the Paperwork Reduction Act of 1995. You do not need to answer these questions unless we display a valid Office of Management and Budget control number. We estimate that it will take about 11 minutes to read the instructions, gather the facts, and answer the questions. SEND OR BRING THE COMPLETED FORM TO YOUR LOCAL SOCIAL SECURITY OFFICE. You can find your local Social Security office through SSA's website at www.socialsecurity.gov. Offices are also listed under U.S. Government agencies in your telephone directory or you may call Social Security at 1-800-772-1213 (TTY 1-800-325-0778). You may send comments on our time estimate above to: SSA, 6401 Security Blvd., Baltimore, MD 21235-6401. Send only comments relating to our time estimate to this address, not the completed form.

CHANGES TO BE REPORTED AND HOW TO REPORT
FAILURE TO REPORT MAY RESULT IN OVERPAYMENTS THAT MUST BE REPAID, AND IN POSSIBLE MONETARY PENALTIES

- You change your mailing address for checks or residence. (To avoid delay in receipt of checks you should ALSO file a regular change of address notice with your post office.)
- Your citizenship or immigration status changes.
- You go outside the U.S.A. for 30 consecutive days or longer.
- Any beneficiary dies or becomes unable to handle benefits.
- Work Changes—On your application you told us you expect total earnings for _____ (year) to be $_____
  - ••You ☐ (are) ☐ (are not) earning wages of more than $_____ a month.
  - ••You ☐ (are) ☐ (are not) self-employed rendering substantial services in your trade or business. (Report AT ONCE if this work pattern changes.)
- Change of Marital Status – Marriage, divorce, and annulment of marriage. You must report marriage even if you believe that an exception applies.
- You are confined to a jail, prison, penal institution or correctional facility for more than 30 continuous days for conviction of a crime, or you are confined for more than 30 continuous days to a public institution by a court order in connection with a crime.
- You have an unsatisfied warrant for more than 30 continuous days for your arrest for a crime or attempted crime that is a felony of flight to avoid prosecution or confinement, escape from custody and flight-escape. In most jurisdictions that do not classify crimes as felonies, this applies to a crime that is punishable by death or imprisonment for a term exceeding one year (regardless of the actual sentence imposed).
- You have an unsatisfied warrant for more than 30 continuous days for a violation of probation or parole under Federal or State law.
- You become entitled to a pension, an annuity, or a lump sum payment based on your employment not covered by Social Security, or if such pension or annuity stops.

- Custody Change or Disability Improves – Report if a person for whom you are filing or who is in your care dies, leaves your care or custody, changes address, or if disabled, the condition improves.
- If you become the parent of a child (including an adopted child) after you have filed your claim, let us know about the child so we can decide if the child is eligible for benefits. Failure to report the existence of these children may result in the loss of possible benefits to the child(ren).
- Your stepchild is entitled to benefits on your record and you and the stepchild's parent divorce. Stepchild benefits are not payable beginning with the month after the month the divorce becomes final.

HOW TO REPORT

You can make your reports online, by telephone, mail, or in person, whichever you prefer.

If you are awarded benefits, and one or more of the above change(s) occur, you should report by:

- Visiting the section "mySocialSecurity" at our web site at www.socialsecurity.gov.
- Calling us TOLL FREE at 1-800-772-1213.
- If you are deaf or hearing impaired, calling us TOLL FREE at 1-800-325-0778; or
- Calling, visiting or writing your local Social Security office at the phone number and address shown on your claim receipt.

For general information about Social Security, visit our web site at www.socialsecurity.gov.

For those under full retirement age, the law requires that a report of earnings be filed with SSA within 3 months and 15 days after the end of any taxable year in which you earn more than the annual exempt amount. You may contact SSA to file a report. Otherwise, SSA will use the earnings reported by your employer(s) and your self-employment tax return (if applicable) as the report of earnings required by law, and adjust benefits under the earnings test. It is your responsibility to ensure that the information you give concerning your earnings is correct. You must furnish additional information as needed when your benefit adjustment is not correct based on the earnings on your record.

Under a special rule known as the Monthly Earnings Test, you can get a full benefit for any month in which you did not earn wages over the monthly limit and do not perform substantial services in self-employment regardless of how much you earn in the year. For retirement age beneficiaries this special rule can be used only for one taxable year which will usually be the year of retirement. For younger beneficiaries such as young wives and husbands (entitled only by reason of child-in-care), this special rule can be used for two taxable years. The first taxable year in which the monthly earnings test may be used is usually the first year they are entitled to benefits. The second taxable year in which the monthly earnings test can be used is always the year in which their entitlement to benefits stops. In all other years, the total amount of benefits payable will be based solely on your total yearly earnings without regard to monthly earnings or services rendered in self-employment.

PLEASE READ THE FOLLOWING INFORMATION CAREFULLY BEFORE YOU ANSWER QUESTION 21.

- If you are under full retirement age, wife's or husband's benefits cannot be paid for any month in which you file your claim.
- If you are full retirement age or older, wife's or husband's benefits may be payable for some months before the month in which you file this claim, but not before the month you attain full retirement age.
- If your first month of entitlement is prior to full retirement age, your benefit rate will be reduced. However, if you do not actually receive your full benefit amount for one or more months before full retirement age because benefits are withheld due to your earnings, your benefit will be increased at full retirement age to give credit for this withholding. Thus, your benefit amount at full retirement age will be reduced only if you receive one or more full benefit payments prior to the month you attain full retirement age.

Chapter Seven

Once You Are Retired

56. What are direct deposit and Direct Express®?

57. How do I sign up for Direct Express®?

58. Can I have direct deposit of my Social Security benefit split between two bank accounts?

59. Can I use direct deposit if I live outside the United States?

60. When will I receive my benefit payment each month?

61. What is the COLA (Cost of Living Adjustment) and what is its history?

62. How much will the COLA amount be for 2018 and when will I receive it?

63. Am I eligible for cost-of-living benefit increases even if I have not started receiving benefits?

64. Can I withdraw my Social Security retirement claim and re-apply later to increase my benefit amount?

65. If I get married, will it affect my benefits?

66. What is the special rule about earnings in the first year of retirement?

67. Are the benefits withheld under the Earnings Test "lost"?

68. How do special payments I got after I retired affect my Social Security retirement benefits?

69. I had additional earnings after I retired; will my monthly Social Security retirement benefit increase?

70. Are there other ways that work can increase my benefits?

71. What happens if I work and get Social Security retirement benefits?

72. Must I pay taxes on Social Security benefits?

73. Must I pay Social Security taxes on my earnings after full retirement age?

74. How can I have income taxes withheld from my Social Security benefits?

75. Will withdrawals from my individual retirement account affect my Social Security benefits?

76. Will unemployment benefits affect my Social Security benefits?

77. Can I transfer future Social Security benefits?

78. How can I get a benefit verification letter?

79. Can my Social Security benefits be garnished for alimony, child support, or restitution?

80. Can my Social Security retirement benefits be levied or garnished to pay student loans?

81. What are the laws allowing the garnishment and levy of Social Security benefits?

82. If I am arrested while on parole or probation, will my benefits stop?

83. What changes do I need to report to Social Security?

84. What should I do when someone who gets benefits dies?

56. What are direct deposit and Direct Express®?

By choosing to get your Social Security or Supplemental Security Income benefits by direct deposit, we will electronically deposit your funds directly into a bank's depository account (e.g. checking account, savings account, and prepaid card account).

By choosing Direct Express*, we will electronically deposit your funds directly into a prepaid debit card account. Direct Express* has no enrollment fee or minimum balance requirement to open or use the account.

57. How do I sign up for Direct Express®?

Signing up is quick and easy. To sign up for a Direct Express® account, you may use one of the three following enrollment options:

- Call the Social Security at 1-800-772-1213,
- Call or visit your local field office (FO), or
- Call Treasury's Direct Express toll free enrollment number (1-800-333-1795) (TTY Line: 1-866-569-0447).

Already Receiving Benefits.

If you already receive Social Security or SSI benefits and you have a bank account, you can sign up for Direct Deposit by:

- Starting or changing Direct Deposit online (Social Security benefits only), or
- Contacting your bank, credit union or savings and loan association, or
- Calling Social Security toll-free at 1-800-772-1213 (TTY 1-800-325-0778), or
- Consider the Direct Express® debit card as another viable option.

The Direct Express® card is a debit card you can use to access your benefits. And you don't need a bank account. With the Direct Express® card program, we deposit your federal benefit payment directly into your card account. Your monthly benefits will be available on your payment day—on time, every time. You can use the card to make purchases, pay bills or get cash at thousands of locations.

It's quick and easy to sign up for the card. Call the toll-free Direct Express® hotline at 1-800-333-1795. Also, Social Security can help you sign up.

About Direct Deposit: If you don't have an account, you must open an account before you can sign up for Direct Deposit. You should shop around in your area to find an account that has the features you want at a price you can afford. Some financial institutions offer a low cost account called an "Electronic Transfer Account." When you decide on the account that is right for you, let the representative at the financial institution know that you are interested in signing up to receive your benefits by Direct Deposit.

Not Currently Receiving Benefits.

If you don't get Social Security or SSI benefits yet but are planning to apply, tell the Social Security representative when you apply for benefits that you want to sign up for Direct Deposit. If you already have an account, have your checkbook or a copy of your bank statement with you.

---

58. Can I have the direct deposit of my Social Security benefit split between two bank accounts?

Currently our system allows direct deposit only to a single account, at a financial institution (e.g. checking account, savings account, and prepaid card account). However, you may preauthorize your financial institution to transfer funds into your other bank accounts.

59. Can I use direct deposit if I live outside the United States?

If you live outside the United States, you can choose to receive your Retirement, Survivors, and Disability Insurance (RSDI) benefits electronically. You can have your benefits sent to a financial institution in the United States or in your country of residence. To receive benefits electronically, you must live in a country where we can send benefits. Special rules apply if you are in a country where we cannot send payments.

60. When will I receive my benefit payment each month?

We pay Social Security benefits monthly. The benefits are paid in the month following the month for which they are due. For example, you would receive your July benefit in August. Generally, the day of the month you receive your benefit payment depends on the birth date of the person on whose earnings record you receive benefits. For example, if you get benefits as a retired worker, we base your benefit payment date on your birth date. If you receive benefits based on your spouse's work, we base your benefit payment date on your spouse's birth date.

Date of Birth	Payment Day
1st–10th	Second Wednesday
11th–20th	Third Wednesday
21st–31st	Fourth Wednesday

[NOTE: If you receive both Social Security and SSI benefits, your Social Security payment will arrive on the third day of the month and your SSI payment will arrive on the first day of the month.]

61. What is the COLA (Cost of Living Adjustment) and what is its history?

Since 1975, Social Security general benefit increases have been cost-of-living adjustments or COLAs. The 1975–82 COLAs were effective with Social Security benefits payable for June in each of those years; thereafter COLAs have been effective with benefits payable for December.

Prior to 1975, Social Security benefit increases were set by legislation.

Social Security Cost-Of-Living Adjustments					
Year	COLA	Year	COLA	Year	COLA
1975	8.0	1990	5.4	2005	4.1
1976	6.4	1991	3.7	2006	3.3
1977	5.9	1992	3.0	2007	2.3
1978	6.5	1993	2.6	2008	5.8
1979	9.9	1994	2.8	2009	0.0
1980	14.3	1995	2.6	2010	0.0
1981	11.2	1996	2.9	2011	3.6
1982	7.4	1997	2.1	2012	1.7
1983	3.5	1998	1.3	2013	1.5
1984	3.5	1999 *	2.5	2014	1.7
1985	3.1	2000	3.5	2015	0.0
1986	1.3	2001	2.6	2016	0.3
1987	4.2	2002	1.4		
1988	4.0	2003	2.1		
1989	4.7	2004	2.7		

* The COLA for December 1999 was originally determined as 2.4 percent based on CPIs published by the Bureau of Labor Statistics. Pursuant to Public Law 106-554, however, this COLA is effectively now 2.5 percent.

The first COLA, for June 1975, was based on the increase in the Consumer Price Index for Urban Wage Earners and Clerical Workers (CPI-W) from the second quarter of 1974 to the first quarter of 1975. The 1976–83 COLAs were based on increases in the CPI-W from the first quarter of the prior year to the corresponding quarter of the current year in which the COLA became effective. After 1983, COLAs have been based on increases in the CPI-W from the third quarter of the prior year to the corresponding quarter of the current year in which the COLA became effective.

62. How much will the COLA amount be for 2018 and when will I receive it?

Monthly Social Security benefits for over 66 million Americans will increase 2.0 percent in 2018. The Social Security Act ties the annual cost-of-living adjustment (COLA) to the increase in the Consumer Price Index as determined by the Department of Labor's Bureau of Labor Statistics.

The increase will begin with benefits that Social Security beneficiaries receive in January 2018.

63. Am I eligible for cost-of-living benefit increases even if I have not started receiving benefits?

You are eligible for cost-of-living benefit increases starting with the year you become age 62. This is true even if you don't get benefits until your full retirement age or even age 70. We add cost-of-living increases to your benefits beginning with the year you reach 62, and up to the year you start receiving benefits.

64. Can I withdraw my Social Security retirement claim and re-apply later to increase my benefit amount?

Unexpected changes may occur after you apply to start your Social Security retirement benefits. If you change your mind, you may be able to withdraw your Social Security claim and re-apply at a future date. However, you must do this within 12 months of your original retirement.

65. If I get married, will it affect my benefits?

If you get Social Security disability or retirement benefits and you marry, your benefit will stay the same. Here's how marriage may affect other benefits:

Supplemental Security Income (SSI)

- If you marry, your spouse's income and resources may change your SSI benefit; or
- If you and your spouse both get SSI, your benefit amount will change from an individual rate to a couple's rate.

Benefits for a widow, divorced widow, widower, or divorced widower

- You cannot get benefits if you remarry before age 60; and
- You cannot get benefits if you are disabled and remarry before age 50.

Divorced spouse's benefits
Generally, your benefits end if you remarry.

Benefits for a child under age 18 or student ages 18 or 19
Benefits end if you marry.

66. What is the special rule about earnings in the first year of retirement?

Sometimes people younger than full retirement age retire in the middle of the year and have already earned more than the yearly earnings limit. There is a special rule that applies to earnings for one year, usually the first year of retirement. Under this rule, you can get a full Social Security benefit for any whole month you are retired, regardless of your yearly earnings.

67. Are the benefits withheld under the Earnings Test "lost"?

It is important to note that any benefits withheld while you continue to work are not "lost." Once you reach NRA (normal retirement age), your monthly benefit will be increased permanently to account for the months in which benefits were withheld.

68. How do special payments I got after I retired affect my Social Security retirement benefits?

After you retire, you may get payments for work you did before you started getting Social Security benefits. Some special payments to employees include bonuses, accumulated vacation or sick pay, severance pay, back pay, stand-by pay, sales commissions, and retirement payments. Or, you might get deferred compensation reported on a W-2 form for one year, but earned in a previous year.

69. I had additional earnings after I retired; will my monthly Social Security retirement benefit increase?

Each year we review the records for all working Social Security recipients to see if additional earnings may increase their monthly benefit amounts. If an increase is due, we figure a new benefit amount and pay the increase retroactive to January following the year of earnings.

70. Are there other ways that work can increase your benefits?

Yes. Each year we review the records for all Social Security recipients who work. If your latest year of earnings turns out to be one of your highest 35 years, we refigure your benefit and pay you any increase due. This is an automatic process, and benefits are paid in December of the following year. For example, in December 2018, you should get an increase for your 2017 earnings if those earnings raised your benefit. The increase would be retroactive to January 2018.

71. What happens if I work and get Social Security retirement benefits?

You can get Social Security retirement benefits and work at the same time. However, if you are younger than full retirement age and make more than the yearly earnings limit, we will reduce your benefit. Starting with the month you reach full retirement age, we will not reduce your benefits no matter how much you earn.

■ We use the following earnings limits to reduce your benefits: If you are under full retirement age for the entire year, we deduct $1 from your benefit payments for every $2 you earn above the annual limit.

For 2018 that limit is $17,040.

■ In the year you reach full retirement age, we deduct $1 in benefits for every $3 you earn above a different limit, but we only count earnings before the month you reach your full retirement age.

If you will reach full retirement age in 2018, the limit on your earnings for the months before full retirement age is $45,360.

Starting with the month you reach full retirement age, you can get your benefits with no limit on your earnings.

72. Must I pay taxes on Social Security benefits?

Some people who get Social Security must pay federal income taxes on their benefits. But no one pays taxes on more than 85 percent of their Social Security benefits.

You must pay taxes on your benefits if you file a federal tax return as an "individual" and your "combined income" exceeds $25,000. If you file a joint return, you must pay taxes if you and your spouse have "combined income" of more than $32,000. If you are married and file a separate return, you probably will have to pay taxes on your benefits.

NOTE: "Combined income" includes your adjusted gross income, tax-exempt interest income, and half of your Social Security benefits.

73. Must I pay Social Security taxes on my earnings after full retirement age?

Everyone working in covered employment or self-employment regardless of age or eligibility for benefits must pay Social Security taxes. However, there are narrow exceptions to paying Social Security taxes that apply at any age, such as an individual who qualifies for a religious exemption.

74. How can I have income taxes withheld from my Social Security benefits?

If you get Social Security, you can ask us to withhold funds from your benefit and we will credit them toward your federal taxes.
You can ask us to withhold federal taxes from your Social Security when you apply for benefits.

If you are already receiving benefits or if you want to change or stop your withholding, you'll need a form W-4V from the Internal Revenue Service (IRS).

You can download the form, or call the IRS toll-free number 1-800-829-3676 and ask for Form W-4V, Voluntary Withholding Request. (If you are deaf or hard of hearing, call the IRS TTY number, 1-800-829-4059.)

When you complete the form, you will need to select the percentage of your monthly benefit amount you want withheld. You can have 7%, 10%, 15% or 25% of your monthly benefit withheld for taxes.

NOTE: Only these percentages can be withheld. Flat dollar amounts are not accepted. If you want to know how much a particular percentage is equal to in dollars, call us at 1-800-772-1213. (If you are deaf or hard of hearing, call our TTY number, 1-800-325-0778.)

Sign the form and return it to your local Social Security office by mail or in person.

75. Will withdrawals from my individual retirement account affect my Social Security benefits?

Social Security does not count pension payments, annuities, or the interest or dividends from your savings and investments as earnings. They do not lower your Social Security retirement benefits.

76. Will unemployment benefits affect my Social Security benefits?

Social Security does not count unemployment benefits as earnings. They do not affect retirement benefits.

However, income from Social Security may reduce your unemployment compensation. Contact your state unemployment office for information on how your state applies the reduction.

77. Can I transfer future Social Security benefits?

No, you cannot transfer your future Social Security benefits to someone else.

78. How can I get a benefit verification letter?

If you need proof you get Social Security benefits, Supplemental Security (SSI) Income, or Medicare, you can request a benefit verification letter online by using your mySocialSecurity account. This letter is sometimes called a "budget letter," a "benefits letter," a "proof of income letter," or a "proof of award letter."

You can also request proof that you have never received Social Security benefits or Supplemental Security Income or proof that you have applied for benefits.

To set up or use your account to get a benefit verification letter, go to "Sign In Or Create An Account."

You cannot request a benefit verification letter online for another person, such as a spouse or child.

If you can't or don't want to use your online account, or you need a letter for someone other than yourself, you can call us at 1-800-772-1213 (TTY 1-800-325-0778), Monday through Friday from 7 a.m. to 7 p.m.

79. Can my Social Security benefits be garnished for alimony, child support, or restitution?

We can withhold Social Security benefits to enforce your legal obligation to pay child support, alimony or restitution. State laws determine a valid garnishment order. By law, we garnish current and continuing monthly benefits. We do not make retroactive adjustments.

You cannot appeal to Social Security for implementing garnishment orders. If you disagree with the garnishment, contact an attorney or representative where the court issued the order.

Delinquent taxes

The Department of the Treasury can withhold Social Security benefits to collect overdue federal tax debts. It can use:

- A Notice of Levy to collect overdue federal taxes under section 6334(c) of the Internal Revenue Code; or
- The Federal Payment Levy Program to collect overdue federal taxes. This allows the Department of Treasury to withhold up to 15 percent of your monthly Social Security benefits until you repay the debt.

You cannot appeal the reduction of a Social Security benefit payment under tax levy to Social Security. Contact the Internal Revenue Service at 1-800-829-7650 to discuss any appeal rights.

Delinquent non-tax debts

The Department of the Treasury can withhold Social Security benefits to collect delinquent non-tax debts owed to other federal agencies under the Debt Collection Improvement Act of 1996 (Public Law 104-134). The Department of the Treasury controls this activity and will contact you if you owe a non-tax debt.

We have no control over this reduction of Social Security benefits, and there is no appeal available under the Social Security Act. If you have questions in this situation, contact Treasury staff at 1-800-304-3107.

80. Can my Social Security retirement benefits be levied or garnished to pay student loans?

Treasury's Financial Management Service can also offset, or reduce, your Social Security benefits to collect debts owed to other Federal agencies, such as student loans owed to the Department of Education.

[EDITOR'S NOTE: Student loans from the government are non-dischargeable, which is to say they cannot be discharged by bankruptcy. Think long and hard before you take out or guarantee a student loan for a child or grandchild, because the Department of Education can always come after your Social Security if they don't get paid!]

81. What are the laws allowing the garnishment and levy of Social Security benefits?

Section 207 of the Social Security Act (42 U.S.C. 407) protects Social Security benefits from garnishment, levy or other withholdings by the federal government, except:

- To enforce child support and alimony obligations under Section 459 of the Social Security Act (42 U.S.C. 659);
- For certain civil penalties under the Mandatory Victim Restitution Act (18 U.S.C. 3613);
- With a Notice of Levy to collect overdue federal taxes under Section 6334(c) of the Internal Revenue Code;

- Through the Federal Payment Levy Program to collect overdue federal taxes by levying up to 15 percent of each monthly payment until the debt is paid under Section 1024 of the Taxpayer Relief Act of 1997 (Public Law 105-34);
- To withhold and pay another federal agency for a non-tax debt you owe to that agency according to the Debt Collection Improvement Act of 1996 (Public Law 104-134).

You can choose for Social Security to withhold a percentage of your benefits to pay to the Internal Revenue Service to satisfy your federal income tax liability for the current year.

82. If I am arrested while on parole or probation, will my benefits stop?

If you get Social Security retirement, survivors, or disability benefits, we will not stop your benefits until a court or parole board cancels your parole or probation, and confines you in a correctional institution for more than 30 consecutive days.

83. What changes do I need to report to Social Security?

Let us know as soon as possible when one of the changes listed in this section occurs.

NOTE: Failure to report a change may result in an overpayment. If you're overpaid, we'll recover any payments not due you. Also, if you fail to report changes in a timely way or you intentionally make a false statement, we may stop your benefits. For the first violation, your benefits will stop for six months; for the second violation, 12 months; and for the third, 24 months.

You can call, write, or visit us to make a report. Have your claim number handy. If you receive benefits based on your work, your claim number is that same as your Social Security number. If you receive benefits on someone else's work record, your claim number will be on any letter we send you about your benefits.

Another government agency may give Social Security information you report to them, but you must also report the change to us.

If your estimated earnings change

If you're working we usually ask you to estimate your earnings for the year. If later you realize your earnings will be higher or lower than you estimated, let us know as soon as possible so we can adjust your benefits.

If you move

When you plan to move, tell us your new address and phone number as soon as you know them. Even if you receive your benefits by direct deposit, Social Security must have your correct address so we can send letters and other important information to you. We'll stop your benefits if we can't contact you. You can change your address at our website by opening a mySocialSecurity account. Or you can call 1-800-772-1213 and use our automated system.

If any family members who are getting benefits are moving with you, please tell us their names. Be sure you also file a change of address with your post office.

If you change direct deposit accounts

If you change financial institutions, or open a new account, you can change your direct deposit online if you have a mySocialSecurity account. Or, we can change your direct deposit information over the telephone after we confirm your identity. Have your new and old bank numbers handy when you call us. These numbers are printed on your personal checks or account statements. This information takes about 30-60 days to change.

Don't close your old account until after you make sure your Social Security benefits are being deposited into the new account.

If a person isn't able to manage funds

Sometimes a person can't manage their own money. If this happens, someone should let us know. We can arrange to send benefits to a relative, other person, or organization that agrees to use the money for the well-being of the person getting benefits. We call this person or organization a "representative payee."

NOTE: People who have "legal guardianship" or "power of attorney" for someone don't automatically qualify to be a representative payee.

If you get a pension from non-covered work

If you start receiving a pension from a job for which you did not pay Social Security taxes—for example, from the federal Civil Service Retirement System or some state of local pension systems—your Social Security benefits may need to be recalculated, and they may be reduced. Also, tell us if the amount of your pension changes.

If you get married or divorced

If you get married or divorced, your Social Security benefits may be affected, depending on the kind of benefits you receive.

If we stop your benefits because of marriage or remarriage, we may start them again if the marriage ends.

The chart (that follows) includes examples:

If you get:	Then:
Your own retirement benefits	Your benefits will continue.
Spouse's benefits	Your benefits will continue if you get divorced and you're age 62 or older unless you were married less than 10 years.
Widow or widower's benefits	Your benefits will continue if you remarry when you are age 60 or older.
Any other kind of benefits	Generally, your benefits will stop when you get married. Your benefits may be started again if the marriage ends.

If you change your name

If you change your name—by marriage, divorce, or court order—you need to tell us right away. If you don't give us this information, your benefits will come under your old name and, if you have direct deposit, payments may not reach your account.

If you get benefits because you are caring for a child

If you receive benefits because you are caring for a child who is younger than age 16 or disabled, you should notify us right away if the child is no longer in your care or changes address. Give us the name and address of the person with whom the child is living.

A temporary separation may not affect your benefits if you continue to exercise parental control over the child, but your benefits will stop if you no longer have responsibility for the child. If the child returns to your care, we can start sending benefits to you again.

Your benefits will end when the youngest unmarried child in your care reaches age 16, unless the child is disabled.

If someone adopts a child who is receiving benefits

When a child who is receiving benefits is adopted, let us know the child's new name, the date of the adoption decree, and the adopting parent's name and address. The adoption won't cause benefits to end.

If you become a parent after you begin to receive benefits

If you become the parent of a child (including an adopted child) after you begin receiving benefits, let us know so we can decide whether the child is eligible for benefits.

If you have an outstanding warrant for your arrest

You must tell us if you have an outstanding arrest warrant for any of the following felony offenses:

- Flight to avoid prosecution or confinement;
- Escape from custody; and
- Flight-escape.

You can't receive regular retirement, survivors, disability benefits, or any underpayments you may be due, for any month in which there is an outstanding arrest warrant for any of these felony offenses.

If you're convicted of a criminal offense

If you get Social Security benefits and are convicted of a crime, Social Security should be notified immediately. Benefits generally aren't paid for the months a person is confined, but family members who are eligible may continue to receive benefits.

If you've committed a crime and are confined to an institution

Benefits usually aren't paid to persons who commit a crime and are confined to an institution by court order and at public expense for more than 30 continuous days. This applies if a person has been found:

- Guilty, but insane; or
- Not guilty by reason of insanity or similar factors (such as mental disease, mental defect, or mental incompetence); or
- Incompetent to stand trial; or
- Sexually dangerous.

If you violate a condition of parole or probation

You must tell us if you're violating a condition of your probation or parole imposed under federal or state law. You can't receive Social Security benefits for any month in which you violate a condition of your probation or parole.

If you leave the United States

If you're a U.S. citizen, you can travel to or live in most foreign countries without affecting your Social Security benefits. There are, however, a few countries where we can't send Social Security payments. These countries are Azerbaijan, Belarus, Cuba, Georgia, Kazakhstan, Kyrgystan, Moldova, North Korea, Tajikistan, Turkmenistan, Ukraine, Uzbekistan and Vietnam. However, we can make exceptions for certain eligible beneficiaries in countries other than Cuba and North Korea. For more information about these exceptions, please contact your local Social Security office.

[EDITOR'S NOTE: this information is accurate as of the time of publication of this book, but the situation vis-à-vis Cuba is changing, so you should also contact your local Social Security office if you're planning to spend time in Cuba.]

Let us know if you plan to go outside the United States for a trip that lasts 30 days or more. Tell us the name of the country or countries you plan to visit and the date you expect to leave the United States. We'll send you special reporting instructions and tell you how to arrange for your benefits while you're away. Be sure to let us know when you return to the United States.

If you aren't a U.S. citizen, and you return to live in the United States, you must provide evidence of your non-citizen status to continue receiving benefits. If you work outside the United States, different rules apply in deciding whether you get your benefits.

If your citizen status changes

If you aren't a citizen, let us know if you become a U.S. citizen or your non-citizen status changes. If your immigration status expires, you must give us new evidence that shows you continue to be in the United States lawfully.

If a beneficiary dies

Let us know if a person receiving Social Security benefits dies. We can't pay benefits for the month of death. That means that if a person died in July, the check received in August (which is payment for July) must be returned. If the payment is by direct deposit, notify the financial institution as soon as possible so it can return any payments received after death.

Family members may be eligible for Social Security survivors benefits when a person getting benefits dies.

If you're receiving Social Security and Railroad retirement benefits

If you're receiving both Social Security and Railroad Retirement benefits based on your spouse's work, and your spouse dies, you must tell us immediately. You'll no longer be eligible to receive both benefits. You'll be notified which survivor benefit you'll receive.

84. What should I do when someone who gets benefits dies?

Notify Social Security as soon as possible when someone getting benefits dies. In most cases, the funeral director will report the person's death to Social Security. Give the funeral director the deceased's Social Security number so he or she can report the death.

Chapter Eight

Recent Changes

What Recent Social Security Claiming Changes Mean for Me

The Bipartisan Budget Act of 2015 (Public Law 114-74; November 2, 2015), made some changes to Social Security's laws about claiming retirement and spousal benefits. Section 831 of the law (entitled "Closure of Unintended Loopholes") made several changes to the Social Security Act and closed two complex loopholes that were used primarily by married couples.

Changes Concerning Deemed Filing for Retirement and Spouse's Benefits

85. What are the changes concerning Timing of Multiple Benefits (also called "deemed filing")?

86. What are the new rules for deemed filing resulting from the Bipartisan Budget Act of 2015?

87. What is the effective date for the new rules on deemed filing resulting from the Bipartisan Budget Act?

88. I turned 62 before January 2, 2016. Does the new law on deemed filing under the Bipartisan Budget Act affect me?

89. Can I restrict my application for benefits and apply only for spouse's benefits and delay filing for my own retirement benefit in order to earn delayed retirement credits?

90. Do the rules for deemed filing apply to all benefits?

Changes Concerning Voluntary Suspension of Benefits (also called "File and Suspend")

91. What are the changes concerning Voluntary Suspension of Benefits (also called "File and Suspend")?

92. What are the new rules for voluntary suspension resulting from the Bipartisan Budget Act of 2015?

93. Will I still be able to file and suspend my benefits in order to receive delayed retirement credits after the effective date for the new rules for voluntary suspension?

94. When do the new rules for voluntary suspension based on the Bipartisan Budget Act of 2015 begin?

95. I have already requested voluntary suspension before April 30, 2016. Will I be affected by the new rules?

96. I am receiving divorced spouse's benefits. If my ex-spouse requests voluntary suspension, will my benefits that I receive on his record be suspended?

85. What are the changes concerning Timing of Multiple Benefits (also called "deemed filing")?

<u>What was the loophole?</u>

The law provides incentives to delay claiming retirement benefits: monthly benefits grow larger for each month you delay receiving retirement benefits between full retirement age (currently 66) and 70. The loophole allowed some married individuals to start receiving spousal benefits at full retirement age, while letting their own retirement benefit grow by delaying it.

<u>How is the law changing?</u>

Under existing law, if you are eligible for benefits both as a retired worker and as a spouse (or divorced spouse) in the first month you want your benefits to begin and are not yet full retirement age, you must apply for both benefits. You will receive the higher of the two benefits. This requirement is called "deemed filing" because when you apply for one benefit you are "deemed" to have also applied for the other.

Under the new law deemed filing is extended to apply to those at full retirement age and beyond. In addition, deemed filing may occur in any month after becoming entitled to retirement benefits. For example, if you begin receiving your retirement benefit and only later become eligible for a spousal benefit (or vice versa), you will be "deemed" to have applied for the second benefit as soon as you are eligible for it. Your monthly payment will be the higher of the two benefit amounts.

<u>What is the rationale for this change?</u>

Historically, spousal benefits were designed to be paid only to the extent they exceeded any benefit the spouse earned based on his or her own work record. This change in the law preserves the fairness of the incentives to delay, but it means that you cannot receive one type of benefit while at the same time earning a bonus for delaying the other benefit.

Who will be affected?

If you turn 62 on or after January 2, 2016, and will be eligible for benefits both as a retired worker and as a spouse (or divorced spouse), then the new law applies to you. Deemed filing applies to retirement benefits, not to survivor's benefits. So, if you are a widow or widower, you may start your survivor benefit independently of your retirement benefit if you restrict the scope of your application. There are also some exceptions to deemed filing. For example, deemed filing does not apply if you receive spouse's benefits and are also entitled to disability, or if you are receiving spousal benefits because you are caring for the retired worker's child. If you have questions about your specific situation, contact Social Security.

How and when is Social Security implementing this change?

We have already implemented this change with specific instructions to our field office employees because the law applies to those who attain age 62 on January 2, 2016, or later. We are continuing to update our website and materials.

Example 1: Maria turns age 62 after January 1, 2016, and her husband, Joe, is 65. They have each worked enough years to earn a retirement benefit. In March of 2020, Maria has reached her full retirement age and files for benefits. Maria is eligible for a spousal benefit on Joe's record. Maria must file for both benefits. She can no longer file only for the spousal benefit and delay filing for her own retirement. She will receive a combination of the two benefits that equals the higher amount.

Example 2: Jennie is a 62-year-old widow. She is eligible for retirement benefits based on her work history, and she is also eligible for survivor benefits based on her deceased husband's record. She starts her survivor benefit this year, restricts the scope of her application to widow's benefits, and does not start her own retirement benefit, allowing it to grow. At age 70, she starts her own increased retirement benefit, which she will receive for the rest of her life. The new law does not affect her because deemed filing does not apply to widow(er)s. Jennie will receive the higher of the two benefits.

86. What are the new rules for deemed filing resulting from the Bipartisan Budget Act of 2015?

Deemed filing means that when you file for either your retirement or your spouse's benefit, you are required or "deemed" to file for the other benefit as well. Deemed filing rules already apply when you file for either your retirement or your spouse's benefit and you are before full retirement age. The Bipartisan Budget Act extends deemed filing rules to apply at full retirement age (FRA) and beyond.

87. What is the effective date for the new rules on deemed filing resulting from the Bipartisan Budget Act?

The new rules for deemed filing are effective immediately for individuals who turn 62 on or after January 2, 2016. An individual born on January 2, 1954 will reach his or her full retirement age (66) in 2020. Therefore, January 2020 is the first month deemed filing will apply to someone who reaches full retirement age. Until that time, deemed filing will only apply to those below full retirement age.

88. I turned 62 before January 2, 2016. Does the new law on deemed filing under the Bipartisan Budget Act affect me?

No, if you turned 62 prior to January 2, 2016, the new law that extends deemed filing rules to benefits at full retirement age and beyond will not apply to you.

89. Can I restrict my application for benefits and apply only for spouse's benefits and delay filing for my own retirement benefit in order to earn delayed retirement credits?

If you turned 62 before January 2, 2016, deemed filing rules will not apply if you file at full retirement age or later. This means that you may file for either your spouse's benefit or your retirement benefit without being required or "deemed" to file for the other. In your case, you may also restrict your application to apply only for spouse's benefits and delay filing for your own retirement in order to earn delayed retirement credits. However, if you turn age 62 on or after January 2, 2016, you are required or "deemed" to file for both your own retirement and for any benefits you are due as a spouse, no matter what age you are.

90. Do the rules for deemed filing apply to all benefits?

No, the rules for deemed filing apply only to retirement benefits based on your own work record and to the spousal benefits (including divorced spouse's) you receive based on retirement. There are two exceptions in which deemed filing does not apply to these benefits. If you receive a spousal benefit because you are caring for a child who is under age 16 or disabled or if you receive spouse's benefits and are also entitled to disability, deemed filing does not apply and you are therefore not required or "deemed" to file for your retirement benefit.

91. What are the changes concerning Voluntary Suspension of Benefits (also called "File and Suspend")?

What was the loophole?

As described above, retirement benefits grow for each month you delay claiming, between full retirement age (currently 66) and 70. A loophole allowed a worker at full retirement age or older to apply for retirement benefits and then voluntarily suspend payment of those retirement benefits, which allowed a spousal benefit to be paid to his or her spouse while the worker was not collecting retirement benefits. The worker would then restart his or her retirement benefits later, for example at age 70, with an increase for every month retirement benefits were suspended.

How is the law changing?
Under the new law, you can still voluntarily suspend benefit payments at your full retirement age (currently 66) in order to earn higher benefits for delaying. But during a voluntary suspension, other benefits payable on your record, such as benefits to your spouse, are also suspended. And, if you have suspended your benefits, you cannot continue receiving other benefits (such as spousal benefits) on another person's record.

There are some exceptions. If you are a divorced spouse, you can continue receiving a divorced spousal benefit even if your ex-spouse voluntarily suspends his or her retirement benefit.

What is the rationale for this change?
There is less rationale for paying dependents if the primary worker has not retired or is not receiving payment from Social Security. It also preserves the fairness of the incentives to delay, so that couples cannot simultaneously receive a benefit and get a bonus for delaying.

Who will be affected?
The new law applies to individuals who request a suspension on or after April 30, 2016, which is 180 days after the new law was enacted. Remember, you must have reached your full retirement age (currently 66) in order to request a suspension.

In some situations, we will honor requests received before April 30, 2016, that we are unable to process until after April 30, 2016. For example, there could be a situation where you are already full retirement age, and you contact us to apply for benefits before April 30, 2016, expressing your intent to apply for, and suspend, your benefits.

If we cannot take your application until June 2016, we will honor the request for voluntary suspension that we received before April 30, 2016.

If you voluntarily suspended benefits prior to April 30, 2016, you may remain in voluntary suspense status, and the new law will not affect you. Also, if you submit your request before April 30, 2016, and your spouse or children become entitled to benefits either before or after that date, they will not be affected by the new rules and will continue to receive payment.

How and when is Social Security implementing this change?
We have developed instructions for our field office employees so they can answer questions before this change takes effect for suspension requests that are submitted on or after April 30, 2016.

Example: Thomas will turn 66 in 2016, and Maria will turn 62. Thomas starts his retirement benefit at his full retirement age, 66, in June 2016, and Maria starts her spousal benefit based on his record. Thomas immediately suspends his benefit. In past years, that would have meant that Maria could continue receiving spousal benefits while Thomas could restart his own benefit at age 70 and receive an increase for each month he waited. Now, because Thomas reached his full retirement age and requested the suspension after April 30, 2016, he is subject to the new law. He can still choose to voluntarily suspend his benefit after his full retirement age, but if he does suspend his benefits, Maria's spousal benefit will also be suspended.

92. What are the new rules for voluntary suspension resulting from the Bipartisan Budget Act of 2015?

If you submit a request to suspend your benefits to earn delayed retirement credits on or after April 30, 2016, you will not be able to receive auxiliary benefits on someone else's Social Security record. In addition, if you suspend your benefit, anyone receiving benefits on your record (excluding divorced spouses) will also be suspended for the same months you request suspension.

Finally, for requests submitted April 30, 2016 and later, payments will be suspended the month following the month in which the request was made and ending with the earlier of the month before the month in which the individual turns age 70 or the month following the month of the request to resume benefits.

93. Will I still be able to file and suspend my benefits in order to receive delayed retirement credits after the effective date for the new rules for voluntary suspension?

Yes, you will still be able to file and suspend your benefits in order to earn delayed retirement credits.

94. When do the new rules for voluntary suspension based on the Bipartisan Budget Act of 2015 begin?

The new rules for voluntary suspension resulting from the Bipartisan Budget Act are effective for requests to suspend benefits submitted April 30, 2016 and later.

95. I have already requested voluntary suspension before April 30, 2016. Will I be affected by the new rules?

No, the new rules will not affect individuals who have already suspended their benefits before April 30, 2016. Also, if you submit your request before April 30th 2016 and your spouse or children become entitled to benefits either before or after that date, they will not be affected by the new rules and will continue to receive payment.

96. I am receiving divorced spouse's benefits. If my ex-spouse requests voluntary suspension will my benefits that I receive on his record be suspended?

No, the new rules for voluntary suspension do not affect divorced spouse's benefits.

Chapter Nine

The Future of Social Security

97. What is the current status of the Old-Age and Survivors Insurance (OASI) Trust Fund?

98. When will the Trust Funds be depleted? What happens then?

99. What are the long-term projections for Social Security?

100. What can be done to improve the long-term prospects for Social Security?

97. What is the current status of the Old-Age and Survivors Insurance (OASI) Trust Fund?

To illustrate the actuarial status of the Social Security program as a whole, the operations of the OASI and DI (Disability Insurance) funds are often shown on a combined basis as OASDI. However, by law, the two funds are separate entities and therefore the combined fund operations and reserves are hypothetical.

At the end of 2016, the OASDI program was providing benefit payments to about 61 million people: 44 million retired workers and dependents of retired workers, 6 million survivors of deceased workers, and 11 million disabled workers and dependents of disabled workers. During the year, an estimated 171 million people had earnings covered by Social Security and paid payroll taxes on those earnings. Total expenditures in 2016 were $922 billion. Total income was $957 billion, which consisted of $869 billion in non-interest income and $88 billion in interest earnings. *[Editor's Note: Income based on taxation of benefits amounted to $31.6 billion.]* Asset reserves held in special issue U.S. Treasury securities grew from $2.813 trillion at the beginning of the year to $2.848 trillion at the end of the year.

(Taken separately OASI) trust fund receipts in 2016 amounted to $797.5 billion, while disbursements totaled $776.4 billion, an increase in trust fund reserves during 2016 of $21.1 billion.

Total receipts during calendar year 2016 included $681.5 billion in payroll tax contributions. . . .

In 2016, the OASI Trust Fund earned $87.0 billion in net interest... The effective annual rate of interest earned by the reserves in the OASI Trust Fund during calendar year 2016 was 3.1 percent. . . .

OASI Total asset reserves as of December 31, 2015, were $2.78 trillion; as of December 31, 2016: $2.801 trillion.

Through the end of 2091, the combined funds have a present-value unfunded obligation of $12.5 trillion.

(Source for above data: *2017 Annual Report of the Board of Trustees*)

98. When will the Trust Funds be depleted? What happens then?

The asset reserves of the OASDI Trust Funds increased by $35 billion in 2016 to a total of $2.85 trillion. The combined trust fund reserves are still growing and will continue to do so through 2021 (at which point the intermediate actuarial estimate* for the balance of the combined reserves is $3 trillion).

Beginning in 2022, the total annual cost of the program is projected to exceed income.

The year when the combined trust fund reserves are projected to become depleted, if Congress does not act before then, is 2034...At that time, there will be sufficient income coming in to pay 77 percent of scheduled benefits.

(Considered separately, the DI (Disability Insurance) Trust Fund reserves become depleted in 2028 and the OASI (Old-Age and Survivors Insurance) Trust Fund reserves become depleted in 2035.)

*See question #99.

99. What are the long-term projections for Social Security?

EDITOR'S NOTE: Social Security does its long-term projections for two time frames: 75 years and the "infinite horizon." The absurdity of attempting to forecast anything 75 years into the future (let alone for the infinite horizon) is obvious. For example, "the estimates in this report (Trustees/2017) assume that the following two provisions will not be implemented: (1) granting legal work and residence status to an expanded group of individuals who entered the country as children (deferred action for childhood arrivals, or DACA) and (2) granting similar status to certain parents of children born in the U.S. or otherwise living in the country legally (deferred action for parents of Americans, or DAPA). Last year's report assumed these two actions would become effective late in 2016..."). Nonetheless, here we go:

(The 2017 Trustees Report) presents three sets of demographic, economic, and program-specific assumptions:

- Alternative II is the intermediate set of assumptions, and represents the Trustees' best estimates of likely future demographic, economic, and program-specific conditions.
- Alternative I is a low-cost set of assumptions—it assumes relatively rapid economic growth, high inflation, and favorable (from the standpoint of program financing) demographic and program-specific conditions.
- Alternative III is a high-cost set of assumptions—it assumes relatively slow economic growth, low inflation, and unfavorable (from the standpoint of program financing) demographic and program-specific conditions.

Based on the Trustees' intermediate assumptions, Social Security's total income for years 2017 through 2021 exceeds its total cost for each year.

The combined reserves are projected to increase from $2.848 trillion at the beginning of 2017 to $3.000 trillion at the beginning of 2022.

Beginning in 2022, annual cost exceeds total income, and therefore the combined reserves begin to decline, reaching $2.607 trillion at the end of 2026.

. . . Based on (5,000 independently generated) stochastic simulations, trust fund asset reserves will become depleted between 2030 and 2043 with a 95-percent probability.

. . . The 95-percent confidence interval for the trust fund depletion year ranges from 2030 to 2043, and there is a 50-percent probability of trust fund depletion by the end of 2034 (the median depletion year).

The year when the combined trust fund reserves are projected to become depleted, if Congress does not act before then, is 2034 . . . at that time, there will be sufficient income coming in to pay 77 percent of scheduled payments.

Through the end of 2091, the combined funds have a present-value unfunded obligation of $12.5 trillion.

(Intermediate, Low, and High-Cost projections come from Table V1.G6. of the Trustees Report.)

2016: Average wage index: $49,364.95/ GDP: $18.569 trillion

Intermediate projections for 2095: Average wage index: $965,223.22/ GDP: $564.614 trillion

Low-cost projections for 2095: Average wage index: $2,447,034.77/ GDP: $1.604.573 quadrillion.

High-cost projections for 2095: Average wage index: $376,451.76/ GDP: $193.948 trillion.

Infinite Horizon Projections

Another measure of trust fund financial status is the infinite horizon unfunded obligation, which takes account of all annual balances. Even those after 75 years. The extension of the time period past 75 years assumes that current-law OASDI program and the demographic and economic and economic trends used for the 75-year projection continue indefinitely.

. . . The OASDI open group unfunded obligation over the infinite horizon is $34.2 trillion in present value, which is $21.7 trillion larger than for the 75-year period.

[EDITOR'S NOTE: The statistics in this "answer" have been gathered from The 2017 Annual Report of the Board of Trustees of the Federal Old-Age and Survivors Insurance and Federal Disability Trust Funds and a July 13, 2017, News Release.]

---

100. What can be done to improve the long-term prospects for Social Security?

Broadly speaking, the approaches that lawmakers can take include increasing revenues from workers and employers by raising the tax rate or the maximum level of taxable earnings, or by dedicating revenues from other sources; lowering benefits for some or all of the beneficiaries by changing certain program parameters; or a combination of these approaches. There are countless variations on these options, including those that vary the timing, magnitude, and other specifics of the change(s) under consideration.*

[EDITOR'S NOTE: This report presents "a broad range of policy options that address Trust Fund solvency and other issues related to Social Security benefits and financing." In great detail!

The report is much too long to reproduce here, so if you'd like to read it, please visit the website. However, these are the areas in which the implications of possible changes are considered:]

- Cost-of-Living (COLA) Adjustment
- Level of Monthly Benefits
- Retirement Age
- Benefits for Family Members
- Payroll Taxes (including maximum taxable)
- Coverage of Employment/ Earnings
- Investment in Marketable Securities
- Taxation of Benefits
- Individual Accounts

*From the 2017 Trustees Report

[EDITOR'S NOTE: On October 25, 2017, The Office of the Chief Actuary published a report entitled Individual Changes Modifying Social Security (https://www.ssa.gov/OACT/solvency/provisions/). This report also provides a Summary of Provisions That Would Change the Social Security Program.]

Afterword: Some Takeaways

The folks who brought this book to fruition are relatively sophisticated on personal finance, but each one expressed surprise about at least one aspect of Social Security or another. Here are a few:

- 40 credits are usually necessary for you to be eligible for retirement benefits. The quarterly minimum earnings to receive one credit in 2018 is $1,320. If you earn $5,280 (4 x $1,320) during the course of the year, you will receive (the maximum) four credits, even if your earnings are not spread out over four quarters.
- The amount of your benefit is determined by your earnings in the 35 years in which you had your highest earnings.
- There is no penalty or fine if you apply for Social Security and are denied (as long as you have filled out your application truthfully). So if in doubt, apply!
- Social Security benefits may be taxable, depending on your earnings.
- If you are turning 65, you should apply for Medicare even if you are not applying for retirement benefits, or you will be subject to penalties. Medicare premiums are automatically deducted from Social Security payments; however, if you are on Medicare but not yet on Social Security, you will pay your premiums directly to Medicare.
- COLAs (Cost-of-Living Adjustments) begin when you reach age 62, whether you have begun taking retirement benefits or not. (The COLA for 2017, payable in 2018, is 2.0%.)
- BEWARE: Your benefits can be garnished if you guarantee a student loan for a child or grandchild and they don't pay.

Sources and Further Reading

By far the most useful book about Social Security is *Get What's Yours: The Revised Secrets to Maxing Out Your Social Security* by Laurence J. Kotlikoff, Philip Moeller, and Paul Solman. (The Revised Edition was published after the 2015 Bipartisan Budget Act, and includes consideration of those very important changes.)

Social Security for Dummies (latest edition) by Jonathan Peterson, AARP Executive Communications Director, is not just for dummies and provides a solid background on how the program works.

For geeks only:

The Online Social Security Handbook
(https://www.ssa.gov/OP_Home%2Fhandbook/handbook.html):
Wherein are found the 2,728 core rules and thousands of codicils that comprise Social Security.

The 2017 Annual Report of the Board of Trustees of the Federal Old-Age and Survivors Insurance and Federal Disability Insurance Trust Funds
(https://www.ssa.gov/oact/tr/2017/tr2017.pdf).

Individual Changes Modifying Social Security
(https://www.ssa.gov/OACT/solvency/provisions/). These changes are also found in the *Summary of Provisions that Would Change the Social Security Program.*